Contents at a Glance

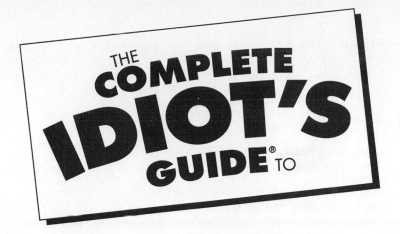

Cleaning

by Mary Findley and Linda Formichelli

ALPHA

A member of Penguin Group (USA) Inc.

This book is dedicated to all my customers, especially those in my early years of cleaning who allowed me to care for their homes, which taught me the knowledge that can be shared now with you.

To Ben and Isabelle

ALPHA BOOKS

Published by the Penguin Group

Penguin Group (USA) Inc., 375 Hudson Street, New York, New York 10014, U.S.A.

Penguin Group (Canada), 10 Alcorn Avenue, Toronto, Ontario, Canada M4V 3B2 (a division of Pearson Penguin Canada Inc.)

Penguin Books Ltd, 80 Strand, London WC2R 0RL, England

Penguin Ireland, 25 St Stephen's Green, Dublin 2, Ireland (a division of Penguin Books Ltd)

Penguin Group (Australia), 250 Camberwell Road, Camberwell, Victoria 3124, Australia (a division of Pearson Australia Group Pty Ltd)

Penguin Books India Pvt Ltd, 11 Community Centre, Panchsheel Park, New Delhi—110 017, India

Penguin Group (NZ), cnr Airborne and Rosedale Roads, Albany, Auckland 1310, New Zealand (a division of Pearson New Zealand Ltd)

Penguin Books (South Africa) (Pty) Ltd, 24 Sturdee Avenue, Rosebank, Johannesburg 2196, South Africa

Penguin Books Ltd, Registered Offices: 80 Strand, London WC2R 0RL, England

International Standard Book Number: 1-59257-487-4
Library of Congress Catalog Card Number: 2005936151

08   07   06   05   8   7   6   5   4   3   2   1

Interpretation of the printing code: The rightmost number of the first series of numbers is the year of the book's printing; the rightmost number of the second series of numbers is the number of the book's printing. For example, a printing code of 05-1 shows that the first printing occurred in 2005

Printed in the United States of America

Note: This publication contains the opinions and ideas of its authors. It is intended to provide helpful and informative material on the subject matter covered. It is sold with the understanding that the authors and publisher are not engaged in rendering professional services in the book. If the reader requires personal assistance or advice, a competent professional should be consulted.

The authors and publisher specifically disclaim any responsibility for any liability, loss, or risk, personal or otherwise, which is incurred as a consequence, directly or indirectly, of the use and application of any of the contents of this book.

Most Alpha books are available at special quantity discounts for bulk purchases for sales promotions, premiums, fund-raising, or educational use. Special books, or book excerpts, can also be created to fit specific needs.

For details, write: Special Markets, Alpha Books, 375 Hudson Street, New York, NY 10014.

Publisher: *Marie Butler-Knight*
Editorial Director/Acquiring Editor: *Mike Sanders*
Senior Managing Editor: *Jennifer Bowles*
Development Editor: *Nancy D. Lewis*
Production Editor: *Megan Douglass*
Copy Editor: *Keith Cline*

Cover Designer: *Bill Thomas*
Book Designer: *Trina Wurst*
Indexer: *Heather McNeill*
Layout: *Ayanna Lacey*
Proofreading: *John Etchison*

Contents

Appendixes

Foreword

Mary Findley is plucky. When I first met Mary, this petite former housecleaner told me she had invented a new mop, starting out in her garage, built a company around it, and was selling these unique terry-cloth-holding mops in surprising numbers to all sorts of people—from maids to motor-home owners. With a dozen types of other mops on the market from as many companies, who would have thought the world needed another mop—and one from the garage of a diminutive cleaning lady? Mary Findley, that's who.

Now, from the knowledge gained in the trenches of her 12 years as a professional housecleaner and more recently as a manufacturer of her own cleaning products, Mary has co-authored her own book, and her passion for changing the way people clean shines through.

Here you'll find advice from scheduling cleaning to selecting a vacuuming cleaner to green cleaning, with lots of Mary's firm-but-gentle cleaning advice included.

Agree or disagree, you'll be moved to look at how you clean and what you clean with (or, in my case, from my lofty perch as an "armchair expert" … what my wife cleans with). Mary's advice on microfiber is a good example. While the world is beating down the doors of stores to buy microfiber cleaning products for every need, Mary says, "be careful, it can damage finished floors and other surfaces" and then persuasively explains why. And what if you don't like store-bought cleaning formulas? Mary's simple recipes for green cleaning products will have you going to the pantry or refrigerator for your cleaning supplies instead of the chemical closet.

Her experience in cleaning large recreational vehicles (RVs) is another example of her can-do spirit, hands-on nature, and hard-earned savvy, and she eagerly shares her tested techniques with readers.

Mary is a dynamo with a joy for cleaning and a love of teaching it, but her experienced co-author Linda Formicelli deserves lots of credit for capturing Mary's spirit and knowledge in a very readable but practical guide that frequently makes readers smile—no small achievement for a book about organizing, dusting, wiping, and mopping.

Formicelli's prose matches Findley's "facts" and style—down to earth, politely powerful, stimulating, surprising, sometimes slightly controversial and edgy—and fun.

In the dusting section, for instance, Formicelli and Findley explain a simple way to dust furniture, advising the unsuspecting reader to get close to the surface, inflate cheeks, think of candles on a cake, purse lips and blow. Thankfully, and more seriously, they explain the importance of using the right tools to avoid creating airborne dust. Black ostrich feather dusters, lambswool, and other tools and techniques are enumerated and detailed.

With all the tips, tricks, and trench-tested advice Mary provides and Formicelli helps package in pithy prose, the reader is not "forced" by dogmatic recommendations, but is provided a bevy of options. Even when it comes to mops—a subject near to Mary's heart as well as her floors—the author provides half a dozen types of mop choices to let the reader choose what fits his or her needs, preferences, and style.

Telling the reader straight and clear what you think in some detail—right or wrong—but letting them make the choice, that's another sign of pluck and caring: a hallmark of Mary Findley the person and professional cleaning expert. Enjoy her book.

Allen Rathey
President of HousekeepingChannel.com

Introduction

You have two choices: you can learn to live with dirt and disorder, or you can spend a bit of time de-cluttering and cleaning your home. If you picked up this book, we're betting you choose the latter!

Even so, we know that many people would rather drive a spike through their forehead than clean the toilet, and if there were a magic button that you could press to have a spanking clean home in an instant, you'd opt for the button over the old-fashioned way. Who wouldn't?

But here's a secret: cleaning can be fun! There's a certain satisfaction in ridding things of dirt and grime and seeing how beautiful they can be, and there's also satisfaction in knowing that you can do this on your own.

This book shows you how to get things their cleanest without spending too much time, energy, or money. You may find yourself going from someone who would rather have that magic button to someone who relishes the idea of making things sparkle!

How This Book Is Organized

This book is organized in four parts.

In **Part 1, "Coming Clean,"** we give you the basics of keeping a clean home. Our tool tips tell you which cleaning products and equipment will help you clean up in a jiffy, and our cleaning schedule gives you the scoop on what you need to clean and how often—so you have an easy reference you can use to remind yourself of daily, weekly, monthly, and yearly tasks. For those of you who are concerned about the environment and your health, our chapter on green cleaning will help you find and create eco-friendly cleaning products.

In **Part 2, "Cleaning House: A Room-By-Room Guide,"** we go through every room of your house, recommending cleaning methods and products for the items in your kitchen, bathroom, living room, and bedroom.

That takes care of much of the little stuff in your home. In **Part 3, "The Big Stuff,"** we help you turn big cleaning challenges into *faits accomplis*—that's French for "a walk in the park." The French also suggest that after you finish these projects—the windows, walls, deck, floors, and more—you go out and treat yourself to a croissant and café au lait.

Finally, in **Part 4, "Other Cleaning Challenges,"** we help you clean everything from electronic gadgets such as cameras and computers to the air you breathe … and our chapter on speed cleaning tells you how to do it all fast. We also give you the 411 on laundry. No more faded brights, pink (former) whites, and sweaters shrunken down to a size that fits your Chihuahua better than it fits a full-grown human. (But doesn't he look cute in argyle!)

Some Things to Help You Out Along the Way

To add to the material in the main text of the book, we've included sidebars that contain items you can use to understand and implement the information in this book.

Mary's Handy Hints

These tips represent Mary's 12 years of cleaning experience. They'll help you make quick work of housework.

Dishing the Dirt

In her years as a cleaning professional, Mary has learned some interesting facts and tidbits. That's what this box is for.

Tidy Terms

These explain definitions of terms used in the text that you might not be familiar with.

Cleaning Quips

Find out what famous writers, actors, and comedians have to say about the art of housework. Some of these will give you a good chuckle as you're cleaning the toilet!

Dirty Words

Warning! Warning! This box contains cautions about cleaning pitfalls that can cause you to lose time, lose money, or worse, lose some of the precious items in your home.

Acknowledgments

Mary's acknowledgments: Nothing is ever achieved without the dedication and assistance of many people.

Linda Formichelli, who patiently guided me through this world of publishing. Your wonderful sense of humor and talented writing skills brought our ideas and knowledge together in a skillful and energetic manner.

Mike Sanders, editor, and Nancy Lewis, development editor, for your insights, dedication, and direction in producing this book.

Paul and Ann Ensch, my parents. You are a constant light in my life. You have guided me, stood by me, and supported me with your love and humor. The solid roots you endowed to me and the wings you set upon my shoulders gave me direction and the path to make this flight.

My husband, Reid. You patiently tolerated my long hours and sometimes grumpy outlook and stepped in to take over our daily living needs. Thank you.

My sister, Nancy White. No words can express the feelings that run so deep in my heart for you. Your wisdom has guided and taught me so much throughout my life.

Paul Ensch, my brother, for your steadfast belief in my abilities and your wonderful sense of humor, and for not letting on to the innumerable times you thought I was out of my right mind for starting this company. Paul, I want to tell you that I lost my right mind a long time ago, and my left mind was never worth a hoot in the first place!

Jason Neland, my son and his loving, beautiful wife, Courtney. I love you both dearly. You are the world to me. I will always be grateful, Jason, for your encouragement along God's path, for your boundless love, and the closeness we share. My special gratitude to you both for presenting me with my granddaughter, Gracie, who already in her short time with us has enriched our lives and touched so many people's hearts.

To my Native Indian elders. Thank you for patiently teaching me to follow the sacred path. For showing me to walk gently on Mother Earth and to search deeply into my spirit to change that which needs changing, nourish that which is good, and forgive what needs to be forgiven.

To my church. Thank you for dedicating your lives to serving God through prayer and service to others. You have been a true inspiration to keep faith, especially when the waters of life turn choppy.

To all of you who have sat through my seminars—many of you several times—and have shared your tips, supported my company, and brought your laughter, hugs, and warmth into my life. You are a true blessing, and I am eternally grateful.

Linda's acknowledgments: I would like to thank the following people who helped make this book—and my writing dreams—come true: co-author Mary Findley; editor Mike Sanders; development editor Nancy Lewis; my agent, Marilyn Allen; my husband, W. Eric Martin; my goal buddy, Jennifer Lawler; my parents, Anthony and Janet Formichelli; and my parents-in-law, Judith and Walter Martin.

Trademarks

Part 1

Coming Clean

They say that it's a poor craftsman who blames his tools. But y'know what? Sometimes the tools are pretty cruddy. In this part, we tell you what tools you need to keep your home sparkling. Then we help you figure out a cleaning schedule that's best for you and your family. After all, it does no good to, say, dust the baseboards every single day but forget to wash the sheets or vacuum the carpets.

If you're worried about the health of the earth—or the health of you and your family—we give you the ins and outs of green cleaning. This includes recipes for all-natural cleaning products that you can brew up in your own kitchen.

Tool Tips

In This Chapter

- ◆ Selecting a vacuum that doesn't suck
- ◆ Choosing cleaning solutions
- ◆ Deciding on dust busters
- ◆ Using rags, cloths, scrubbers, and sponges
- ◆ Sweeping you off your feet: brooms and mops

Your cleaning is only as good as your tools. For example, suppose you clean your floor with a mop that's been around since the Eisenhower administration. Your floor will soon look like it's from that era! Or if you use some cheapo feather duster from the dollar store to dust your nice furniture ... well, those plastic "feather" spines can scratch your furniture. Not exactly the effect you were looking for.

The right tools can make cleaning not only more efficient, but also more fun. (That's right, we said cleaning can be fun!) After all, would you rather use a nasty string mop or a fancy one that has a bottle of cleaning solution attached? Would you rather lug your cleaning materials from place to place in a torn-up plastic bag or in a cool caddy with a place for everything?

In this chapter, we give you the ins and outs of the various tools you need to keep your home as clean as a G-rated movie.

Nature Abhors a Vacuum (but Not Us!)

A vacuum that sucks is an important tool to have in your home. Before beginning your search for a vac, read a consumer guide such as *Consumer Reports* for recommendations. Decide which attachments are essential, such as upholstery brushes and drapery attachments.

Filter It Out

The filtering system in a vacuum is key ... after all, what's the point of cleaning your floor with a vacuum that spews dust out the back? High-efficiency particulate air (or HEPA) filters are expensive to replace, but they do the best job of trapping dust particles, which is essential for anyone with allergies or asthma. Microfiltration systems are an improvement over filterless systems, although they're not as thorough as HEPA filters.

Mary's Handy Hints

Janitorial supply stores that carry vacuums can be a wonderful resource for you—and you don't even have to be a janitor. After looking at residential vacuums, you may decide a commercial vacuum would best suit your needs.

Upright Vacs

Upright vacuums are easier to store than canister vacs (which we discuss next), and you might prefer pushing an upright to tugging a canister vac around behind you as you clean. Some salespeople will tell you that an upright gives you more suction than a canister. In years past this was true, but canisters have changed their features and are now as powerful as uprights.

Canister Vacs

Canisters take up more room in the closet than upright vacs, but they have an automatic retrieval system for the cord that makes rewinding the cord a snap. No more winding the cord around (and around and around) on its holder!

And unlike upright vacs, you don't need to assemble a tube when you find cookie crumbs on the couch left by your youngster. You can purchase additional lengths of tubing if you have a bad back and need the extra length to take the pressure off your back. Canisters are also easier and less taxing on your back when it comes to cleaning the stairs.

Backpack Vacs

Janitorial supply stores carry backpack vacs. Although they're excellent in office buildings, some of the larger models are far too cumbersome for a residential home.

Shopping for a Vacuum

When shopping for a vacuum, take it for a good test run up and down the aisle (making the appropriate "vroom, vroom" noises if you wish) as far as the cord will reach, particularly if there is a hard floor surface close by you can test it on. Most homes have both carpet and hard floor surfaces, and you need an equal feel for both surfaces.

Here are some more issues to consider when looking at vacuums:

◆ Does the vacuum kick dirt out the back? If so, well, that seems pretty pointless, doesn't it?

◆ Is there a manual switch to take you from carpets to a hard floor surface?

◆ Don't hesitate to sit on the floor to take a good look under the hood. How easy is it to remove the *beater bar* to change the belt?

◆ Is there a lot of dust and dirt around the beater bar? If so, that could be an indication that the suction is not up to snuff.

◆ Take a look at the disposable bags. Does the bag look like it's worn along the seam lines? Is there dust or dirt on the outside of the bag? Is there any dust on the inside of the canister that holds the bag?

Tidy Terms

A **beater bar** is a rigid bar in a vacuum that agitates and loosens the dirt in a carpet.

These are all indications that you'll have dust (and goodness knows what else) flying everywhere in your home.

You want a vacuum that doesn't suck, by which we mean a vacuum that sucks ... er, what we're trying to say is ... oh, never mind! Just follow these tips to find the right vac for your home.

Cleaning Solutions

If you're like most people, you have a jumble of dozens of bottles of various cleaning solutions cluttering up your cabinets and closets, making you look more like a mad scientist than a cleaning-conscious housekeeper. Read on to find out which products you really need to get your house sparkling.

Keep in mind that if the product you already have works great and you like it, there's no need to replace it. But if it leaves much to be desired, you can try our homemade solutions from Chapter 3.

Dirty Words _____

If your home is on a septic system, don't use antibacterial soap, shampoo, liquid dish soap, or laundry detergent. The residue in your septic system depends on enzymes to break down solid waste. Antibacterial soaps and detergents kill the enzymes, destroying this natural process.

Tidy Terms _____

By **all-purpose cleaner,** we mean either the homemade recipe in Chapter 3, a concentrated orange-based cleaner such as Bi-O-Kleen or Bio Ox, or a general all-purpose cleaner from the supermarket.

♦ A window cleaner that you can also use to clean mirrors.

♦ *All-purpose cleaner*, which makes short work of dirt and germs on toilets, showers, tubs, sinks, and kitchen counters. This shouldn't be used, however, on granite, marble, or tile counters because any cleaner containing phosphorous or citric acid will deteriorate stone. Acidic cleaners, including white vinegar, damage the finish on marble and granite and "pit" tile. Use hot water only on stone surfaces.

♦ A gentle scouring product such as Bon Ami or Barkeeper's Friend.

♦ All-natural dishwashing detergent that does not contain phosphates. We recommend this because phosphates cause a multitude of problems, mold being one of them. Many states have banned products containing phosphates.

♦ White vinegar. You can use this wonder stuff to clean everything from toilets to windows!

♦ Baking soda for scrubbing toilets, cleaning drains, and more.

That's all you need! Notice that we don't have toilet bowl cleaner, dusting aids, or air fresheners on the list. In this book, you'll learn quick and easy ways to get your home fresh and clean without the need for these expensive products.

Dusters

Here's an easy way to rid your furniture of dust. Ready? Get really close to the furniture, so your face is right next to it. Now, purse your lips and blow like it's your birthday and you're blowing out candles. Voilà! In between sneezing fits, you'll see that your furniture is dust free.

That technique not right for you? Then check out these handy tools.

Feather Dusters

Your best buy is an ostrich feather duster. Remember that real ostrich feathers are black. Those cheapie fake, colorful feather dusters can scratch up your furniture with their plastic spines.

Dusting Cloths

Old but clean 100 percent cotton T-shirts, clean white tube socks, or 100 percent cotton baby diapers make the best dusters. There is a specialty dusting cloth called Kozak (see Appendix B for buying details) that also does a super job. It's a specially treated 100 percent cotton cloth that retains dust efficiently. It is not washable, but it lasts for 40 to 50 dustings. You might want to buy the larger size and cut it in half.

Through the magic of mathematics, you'll then have enough for 80 to 100 dustings!

And let us not forget lambswool; it is hard to beat for dusting cobwebs and dashboards in cars.

Rags, Cloths, Scrubbers, and Sponges

It may be hard to believe that we have to talk about things such as rags and sponges here. After all, just rip up your spouse's hideous old "I'm With Stupid" T-shirt, and voilà! Dusting rags.

But there's much, much more to it than that. Read on for the pros and cons of different choices.

Microfiber: Wonder Material?

Microfiber cloths are marvelous for many uses. Dampened, they quickly remove pet hair and surface dirt from fabric furniture and do a good job removing some food stains from carpeting. They're unbeatable for cleaning windows, mirrors, and computer or TV screens. Keep them handy for wiping down glass shower doors.

Most cleaning books on the market tout the wonders of microfiber towels. A closer look at the fabric will tell you to *caveat emptor*, which is Latin for "It can wreck your furnishings." Microfiber cloths are made from 80 to 85 percent polyester, which is plastic. Polyester made great loungewear in the '70s, but it makes lousy cleaning cloths for many surfaces. Plastic will scratch the sealant or coating off any surface with repeated use.

Rule of thumb for using microfiber: if the surface is sealed, contains any kind of hard coat finish, or is painted, do not use microfiber to dust or clean regularly. This applies to marble, granite, and Corian as well as wood, laminates, and painted surfaces (including walls).

Microfiber comes in various grades. The higher grades are more expensive, but you'll be pleased with their performance. Lower grades, although cheaper, tend to leave lint, are not nearly as absorbent, and don't launder nearly as well as the better grades.

Plain Old Cotton

One hundred percent cotton rags are the safest way to clean. Hand towels that are no longer being used in the bathroom make wonderful rags for kitchen and bathroom duty. They're unbeatable for mopping floors. A pair of scissors and a sewing machine quickly turns a large bath towel into three good rags. Hem the cut edges to prevent raveling. To clean windows, go for 100 percent cotton baby diapers or lint-free towels.

Dry Sponges

Chemically treated dry sponges first made their appearance in the jan san (that's fancy talk for janitorial sanitation) industry for removing soot from walls after a fire. Their popularity has blossomed into the retail market. Use them dry for removing pet hair from furniture, surface cleaning fabric furniture, and cleaning lampshades. They do an excellent job on clothing, too, and work in the car to quickly remove dust and dirt from seats. RVers love them for dusting and cleaning fabric blinds (also called day/night shades) and for their carpeted ceilings.

If you have a spill that needs a fast pickup, grab a dry sponge. They are remarkable at holding liquid. Wash in sudsy water to clean them and air dry. (It takes a few days for them to dry because of their density.)

Scrubbers and Brushes

You'll need several brushes (and a scrubber) to complete your cleaning chores.

Here are the types of scrubbers and brushes you'll need:

- ◆ White nylon scrubbing pads; the blue or green ones can scratch surfaces.

- ◆ An old toothbrush. (No, you can't use your partner's, no matter how mad you are at him or her.) Toothbrushes are great for getting at hard-to-reach areas such as behind the bathroom faucets, in the grout lines in the tub, and in that little groove between the stainless steel sink and the kitchen counter.

- Toilet bowl brushes are either cotton swab type brushes or bristles. Use a brush that does not contain metal parts that can scratch the toilet or rust.

- Kitchen brushes. The most often used are brushes for pots and pans, sink cleaning brushes, and bottle brushes for narrow openings. Curved bottle brushes are wonderful for cleaning refrigerator coils (which should be done every four months).

- Handheld floor brushes for those extra tough cleaning jobs. Be sure to buy kneepads if you'll be on your hands and knees scrubbing the floors!

Dirty Words

You can find grout cleaning brushes on the market, but we've found that they don't just clean the grout—they can remove it entirely! It is best to use a product called The StainEraser (see Appendix B).

- Threaded nylon brushes for stripping floor wax.

- A wire brush for cleaning barbeque grills (stainless steel or copper, for example).

- Paint brushes for cleaning pleated lampshades or getting into nooks and crannies such as the corners of windows. The 1-inch and ½-inch sizes are best for this.

- A horsehair brush to bring the nap back up on furniture made from ultra suede or other similar fabrics.

- A ceiling fan cleaning brush.

- A mini-blind cleaning brush.

If you're the type of person who uses brushes only on your hair and your teeth, get thee to a cleaning supply store or a hardware store and stock up on these cleaning brushes!

A Clean Sweep: Brooms

Need to sweep some dirt under the rug? This section is for you. It's best to use a 100 percent cotton dust mop on hardwood, laminated, marble, or granite flooring. Brooms with bristles can scratch these surfaces. Bristled sweeping brooms, however, do a good job scooting dirt out from the grout of tiled floors.

For homes with large floor surfaces, head to a janitorial supply store for an 18-inch-wide dust mop. Be sure to get an extra replacement head. These are washable and dust large areas quickly.

If you thought electric toothbrushes were a marvelous invention, wait till you hear about electric brooms! They're lightweight and easy to use for light cleaning jobs. Just make sure that if it has a beater bar, it can be raised for hard floor surfaces. These brooms are wonderful for a quick buzz over a floor.

Swabbing the Deck: Mops

Shopping for a mop can be as confusing as shopping for a car. So many models! So many features! So many prices! The only thing missing is the hard-sale pitch.

Here are the pros and cons of the different kinds of mops. They should help you decide on the kind of mop that's best for your floors.

Cotton String Mops

Cotton string mops do very well on tile and slate floors and linoleum, but should never be used on wood or laminated floors. They leave excess moisture on the floor that will warp the boards. Hang your cotton string mop outside to dry even in the dead of winter. The fibers will freeze, but they'll be dry within a few days. (Ever hear of freeze-dried coffee?) Many of our Canadian and Alaskan friends dry their clothes this way.

Sponge Mops

Sponge mops are handy for cleaning spills because the sponges quickly pick up liquids. The heads on sponge mops need to be replaced at least once a month, so buy extra when you get one. Dry any floor immediately after mopping to prevent water-spot damage. Clean in small sections, drying as you go.

Twist Mops

These mops actually do the twist … just put on the appropriate music. Really, they're called twist mops because you twist the mop to wring out the water. Clean all floors in sections and dry as you mop. The heads are machine washable, but be sure to air dry only unless they're 100 percent cotton and completely removable from their plastic holder. Otherwise, the plastic will melt and ruin your dryer, and non-cotton fibers will shrink.

Towel Mops

Towel mops use ordinary terry towels to clean the floor. They're safe for all floor surfaces because limited amounts of water remain on the towel. You can clean the towels each time you use them so the floors aren't recontaminated with the dirt you took off them last week. Replacement costs are minimal—you can even use hand towels that you've retired from the bathroom. They can also be used for dusting cobwebs, washing walls, or cleaning ceilings.

Cleaning Quips

"Housekeeping ain't no joke."

—Louisa May Alcott

Cotton Pad Mops

Flat mops with 100 percent cotton pads can be used safely on all floor surfaces—just be sure to wring out all excess moisture when using on marble or wood floors, the same as you do with towel mops. These easily clean under low areas such as sofas and chairs if you have hard floor surfaces throughout the home.

Microfiber Mops

Microfiber mops should never be used on laminated, wood, marble, granite, or other flooring that is sealed or finished. They are safe to use on tile or slate floors. They're unbeatable in institutional or commercial settings where the floors are continuously buffed and waxed.

Predampened Towelette Mops

The towels are so thin that they have to use a pretty strong cleaner to get the floor clean. Those cleaners are difficult, if not impossible, to rinse from a floor. After you mop the floor and walk over it, it will feel sticky underfoot. That sticky residue builds up, softening the sealant, and it will ruin the finish. Besides, it's extremely expensive to keep replacing the towels. You use three or four of them for one cleaning and all those chemical-laden towels are now being dumped into the landfills. We've received e-mail from users asking how to restore the color to the edges of their carpet after they have used these mops.

Mops with Cleaning Bottles Attached

People have reported they just love the convenience of these mops. You can make your own solution for them with ¼ cup white vinegar and a teaspoon of borax per quart of water. Use only water for any kind of stone floor tile, marble, or granite, and no borax on laminated or wood floors.

The Least You Need to Know

♦ Cheap or inappropriate tools can make your cleaning job much more difficult.

♦ You don't need as many cleaning solutions as you think. Sometimes a sprinkle of baking soda will do the job!

♦ Be sure to test out vacuums and give them a thorough inspection in the store to make sure you wind up with one that sucks (or, rather, that doesn't suck).

♦ Your choice of mop depends on your floor surfaces to be cleaned. A cotton terry towel mop works on most surfaces.

Chapter **2**

Creating a Cleaning Schedule

In This Chapter

- ◆ Understanding why you need a cleaning schedule
- ◆ Creating a schedule that works for you
- ◆ Minding the little stuff: daily and weekly to-dos
- ◆ Tackling the big stuff: twice-monthly to yearly chores

Imagine if trains didn't run on schedules. To get anywhere, you have to show up at the station really early, cross your fingers, and hope a train comes by in time for you to reach your appointment. Or consider what would happen if television networks operated without schedules. Chances are you'd turn on the television hoping to catch *Survivor*, but end up vegging out to a Lawrence Welk retrospective.

Okay, so you get the idea: schedules are vital. Without them, the whole world would turn into a big ball of free-floating chaos and we'd all be rioting in the streets. More importantly, no one would ever get to see *Survivor*.

What does this have to do with cleaning? Much as the world would turn to chaos without train and TV schedules, your home would be pretty chaotic without a cleaning schedule. Sans schedule, you could easily ignore periodic jobs such as dusting the baseboards or vacuuming under heavy furniture because other obligations get in the way. Then, all of a sudden, dust bunnies the size of bowling balls start rolling out from underneath the couch and attacking the dog.

A schedule does more than prevent chaos from taking over your home—it also helps you to incorporate cleaning into your daily life. When cleaning becomes automatic, you'll find yourself zipping through those chores with lightening speed.

In this chapter, we tell you which chores need to go on your schedule and how often you need to do them.

The Scheduling Countdown

A cleaning schedule isn't like a pair of tights in which one size fits all. Everyone's home is different, from the style of curtains in the living room to the number of glass doodads from vacations in other states. Before you can schedule your cleaning schedule (so to speak), you need to survey the interior and exterior of your home and write down:

- ◆ **All the areas that need cleaning.** This one's pretty simple: If you can see it, you need to clean it. Scan each room from top to bottom so you don't miss door frames, pictures, windowsills, mirrors, and baseboards. Different items in the same room will likely be cleaned at different rates, but right now just worry about jotting everything down.

- ◆ **Items that can be stored behind glass.** Small ceramic figurines and other tiny decorative objects take considerable time to clean, but if you can stick them in a glass cabinet, you'll have to clean them only three or four times per year. Beats having to dust them every week with a feather duster—and inevitably knocking one over and breaking it.

- ◆ **How frequently you (really) need to clean each room.** Formal living rooms, dining rooms, and spare bedrooms, to pick some obvious examples, may get by with a monthly cleaning if they're used only on special occasions or while you have visitors. With rooms such as these, you can rotate them on a weekly cleaning schedule so that each is cleaned once a month. This will leave additional time for other, more pertinent cleaning chores and prevent you from putting them off entirely if you penciled them all in on a single day.

◆ **Who in your family can do which job.** Do you have a partner, kids, or a roommate? Put 'em to work! Everyone in a household contributes to the making of messes, so by the same token, everyone should pitch in to clean up. Even small children can help pick up toys (especially if you make a game of it).

Naming Names and Handing Out Tasks

When you have these notes in hand, you're ready to create a schedule that takes into account every area of your home and that works for you and your family.

How do you actually create a cleaning schedule? Any way you like—as long as you'll stick to it. If you have the aforementioned partner, kids, or roommate, you can do an old-fashioned chore wheel in which each person has certain responsibilities that rotate after a set length of time.

Or how about a twist on ye olde job jar? Create different jars for daily, weekly, twice-monthly, quarterly, and yearly tasks, and have your helpers draw jobs from the jar at the appropriate times. It feels like a lottery, and everyone gets to share the prize of living in a tidy home.

If nothing else, you can turn to the timekeeping method of choice for the past 15,000 years: the calendar. You might consider purchasing a birthday calendar (one that lists the dates and months but not the specific days of the week) and devote that to your cleaning schedule. Fill in tasks for the whole year, and when you reach December 31, all you have to do is flip back to the beginning and start again.

Not sure which task goes where? Read on for the breakdown of when and why you do what.

Daily Duties

During each 24-hour period, you'll face a dozen little tasks that require no more than a few minutes of your time. Spending those minutes, however, is key to keeping your home from becoming a disaster. What's more, the minutes you spend now will save hours from the weekly cleaning tasks to come.

- If you haven't developed the habit of putting things away as you finish using them—start now! Don't place something on the counter and promise to put it away later. Put your hands back on it and find it a proper home, be it cabinet, drawer, or dustbin.

- Air the beds. We hear that you lose a horrific amount of fluid through sweat when you sleep, and although some of that surely evaporates in the air, more than you want to think about ends up in your bed. Throw back the sheets and covers, open a window, and let the beds air while you shower and eat breakfast.

- Make the beds. True, you could just shut the bedroom doors and no one else would ever notice, but retiring to a neat room each night is always rewarding. Instead of a crumpled mess that reminds you of last night's nightmare, you're treated to an unblemished surface just waiting for you to dive in and relax.

- Rinse the dishes and put them in the dishwasher after every meal. Each family member should be responsible for rinsing his or her own dishes. (Anyone who disagrees with this policy must go without any dishes at all. No utensils either. If they don't want to clean it, they shouldn't use it.)

Mary's Handy Hints

Refill your spray bottles after you finish cleaning. Then should a spill arise, the bottle (and the bottle-wielder, a.k.a. you) will be ready for fast action.

- Keep a spray bottle of all-purpose cleaner under the sink along with a clean rag. (We recommend filling a clean 32-oz. spray bottle nearly full with water, then adding ⅓ cup of white vinegar and a small squirt of liquid dishwashing detergent.) Clean the stove top every night after dinner. If food has baked onto the surface, squirt it down, finish the dishes, and then wipe the spot clean.

◆ Each night clean one additional kitchen surface such as a countertop, the microwave, cabinet doors, or the top of the refrigerator. By the end of the week, you'll have cleaned the entire kitchen and spent just two or three minutes per night.

◆ Start a load of laundry right before you make dinner. You'll probably be able to switch the load from the washer to the dryer before everything's out of the oven. By the time dinner ends, the clothes will be dry. Clean out the lint trap in your dryer after every load.

◆ Vacuum or sweep high-traffic floors. If your household includes animals of any sort, whether dogs, cats, or rambunctious 12-year-olds, you'll want to keep fur and dirt from spreading from entryways to other parts of the house.

◆ Take out the day's trash each evening. That way you'll wake to a nice, fresh-smelling kitchen!

◆ At the end of every day, toss the day's newspaper and junk mail into the recycling bin. You're finished with it, so don't leave it lying around and force yourself to handle it again tomorrow. (If you really need something in the paper, tear out that item or story and toss everything else.)

The idea behind most daily chores is to get a simple task out of the way as soon as possible so that when you reenter a room, you don't shudder and say, "Oh, yes, I meant to do that before." The work is all in the past, which allows you to concentrate on enjoying the present!

Weekly Work

As you proceed through this chapter, you'll notice that the chores get bigger and more involved the less often you have to do them. Weekly chores are more heavy duty than daily chores, for example, and twice-monthly chores will be heavier still. By the time you get to the yearly tasks, we'll have you pushing boulders up hills!

More seriously, even though a chore is listed in the weekly section, you might get away with doing it less often. In some homes, cleaning the bathrooms and dusting require attention only every other week. If this is true for your home, you can schedule the dusting for one week and the bathrooms for the next.

- Change and launder sheets and pillowcases. We discuss laundry in Chapter 14.

- Go through the refrigerator and toss out anything that has green stuff sprouting or smells like, well—look, just get it out of your fridge before you do the weekly shopping and pile good stuff on bad. For more on cleaning the fridge, follow the instructions in Chapter 5.

- Get a clean damp cloth, squirt on a bit of liquid dish soap, and wipe around cabinet pulls. Oil from your hands quickly deteriorates most sealants, so cleaning the cabinet pulls weekly can eliminate the need for an expensive refinishing job.

 Dirty Words _____

Don't use microfiber products on nonglass items! Although microfiber has been touted as a miracle cloth, it's made mostly from plain ol' polyester. Microfiber needs only water to clean because the plastic scratches off the dirt—but plastic isn't smart enough to know where the dirt ends and the good stuff begins. Over time, it will remove the sealant from any surface, including hardwood floors, cars, and cabinets.

- If you don't clean sections of the kitchen nightly, as we recommended in the "Daily Duties" section, then add kitchens to your weekly to-do list, following the instructions in Chapter 4.

- Even if you don't need to clean your bathrooms every week, you'll still want to spot clean them, making special note of toilets and counters. Otherwise, clean the bathrooms following the instructions in Chapter 5.

- If you live in a dusty area, say in the desert or near a dust factory, weekly dusting is a must. Sand and dust quickly accumulate in the grains of wood, drying and cracking it, but regular care will keep it in tip-top shape.

◆ Sweep and damp mop hard floor surfaces. Instructions for floor care are in Chapter 9.

◆ Clean the blinds or day/night shades in one or two rooms each week depending on the number of blinds in your home.

Some people prefer to scatter these cleaning jobs throughout the week rather than cram them all into a single day or weekend. If you fit this description, decide which day you'll dust, clean bathrooms, vacuum, and damp mop the floors, and then stick to that schedule.

Mary's Handy Hints

Here's a tip for cleaning those pesky Venetian blinds: barely dampen an old sock, put it over your hand, and run your besocked hand between the slats in the blinds.

Twice-Monthly Tasks

Twice monthly, every two weeks, you need to do these tasks approximately every fourteen days to keep your home in tip-top shape.

◆ Clean the bathrooms following the instructions in Chapter 5.

◆ Most homes can get away with a dusting every other week. If yours is one of them, consider alternating dusting weeks with bathroom cleaning weeks to spread out the work.

◆ Thoroughly vacuum carpeted rooms. We discuss vacuuming in Chapter 9.

◆ Clean the drip pans on your stove and both sides of the stove hood.

◆ Clean the formal rooms and any other room that isn't used on a regular basis. See Chapter 7 for information on how to clean living areas.

With these twice-monthly tasks and the infrequent cleaning jobs to come in later sections, it's easy to push them off to another day instead of doing them and marking them off your calendar. Try not to push them back; the more you delay, the more likely you are to have projects pile up on one another—which will make you feel stressed, and even more prone to delay!

Monthly Missions

Some of these tasks are ones that you may not normally think of—until they go undone for so long that you *have* to notice them!

- Sweep the garage, patio, sidewalks, and other outdoor areas. You might think that rain showers keep them clean, but rain brings in as much dirt as it washes away.

- Clean the patio furniture during the months when it's in use. We discuss this in Chapter 11.

- Dust for cobwebs inside the house.

- Dust the baseboards.

- Change or clean furnace filters. Do this monthly if the air conditioner or furnace is running, and once per quarter in the off seasons.

- Use drain opener to keep water flowing smoothly through your pipes. To do this, dump 1 cup of baking soda down the drain, followed up by 1 cup of white vinegar. Wait a couple of hours, then flush with hot water. If you think mold is building up in your drains, add hydrogen peroxide instead of vinegar. Do not use this mixture in kitchen sinks with garbage disposals; instead, use a product called Nature's Miracle, which you can find in pet stores. It contains enzymes that "eat" the gunk in your drain, especially food particles (how appetizing!). Nature's Miracle can be used in all the drains of your home and won't harm sewer and septic systems.

- Wipe off fabric furniture using a dry sponge. These sponges work wonderfully for cleaning cloth shades as well.

- Dust wall hangings.

You can spread these chores out on the calendar so that you tackle one or two per week, or else you can gather the entire family together once a month for an intensive all-day cleaning fest.

Dirty Words _____

Avoid using a hose to sweep your driveway and sidewalk. Not only does this practice waste precious water, you'll actually spend more time running water through the hose than you would hanging on to the end of a broom. The same typically applies to electric or gas-powered leaf blowers. You'll save money and get some exercise by gathering leaves the old-fashioned way!

Quarterly Quagmires

If you're self-employed like your humble authors, you have to pay taxes on a quarterly basis because Social Security taxes aren't withheld from your paychecks. When you take the time to write out that check to Uncle Sam, you should go ahead and write off the rest of the day as well and do your quarterly chores at the same time.

Not self-employed? Thank your lucky stars you don't have to pay quarterly taxes, and schedule your quarterly cleaning tasks for January, April, July, and October.

◆ Clean kitchen and bathroom cabinets with a cleaner made especially for wood.

◆ Remove cobwebs from the eaves of the house. You can either get a broom out and bat away at the cobwebs, getting them in your eyes and hair, or you can grab a mop with an extension handle and an old but sturdy terry towel. Extend the handle, toss the towel over the mop head, and have at the cobwebs. Cobwebs stick to your towel rather than your hair.

◆ Wipe down walls for fingerprints using a natural dish soap (the conventional kind leaves gummy residue that can build up) or a product such as *Non TSP*. Non TSP is nontoxic and safe to use in the home.

◆ Clean windows when necessary. We discuss window washing in Chapter 11.

Tidy Terms _____

Non TSP is a cleaner that doesn't contain harmful trisodium phosphate (TSP).

◆ Clean light fixtures as needed. Some glass light fixtures can be removed and carefully washed in the sink. If you can't remove the fixture from the wall or ceiling, it's probably attached with hinges. Dampen one rag with your all-purpose cleaner and leave another rag dry. Toss one rag over each shoulder. Clean the bottom side of the fixture while it's still in place. Then loosen the screw and gently lower the glass to clean the other side.

◆ Vacuum and clean refrigerator coils and filters. Use a curved drain cleaner brush to thoroughly clean them; brushes on vacuums don't reach all the way through the coils, and the more schmutz on the coils, the less efficient your fridge will be.

◆ Clean ceiling fans. If they can put a man on the moon, why can't they make a tool that will let you clean ceiling fans without climbing a ladder? Oh, wait, they did—it's a special duster on an extension pole. Most stores that sell ceiling fans sell these tools. They are flat and bent to reach over and under the blade with a cleaning cloth that is machine washable. After cleaning the fan with this special duster, take an old cotton tube sock lightly sprayed with water and pull it over a lambswool or other fuzzy duster to clean the base of the fan.

Mary's Handy Hints

Remember to stay focused on the chore at hand. If you work outside your home, then do the laundry either as you get ready for work in the morning or during dinner. Washing clothes as you do other housework slows down your efforts; every time you stop to load or unload a machine, it takes time to get back up to speed.

◆ Remove the contents of one section of your kitchen cabinets, toss anything unused and funky, and clean the shelves.

◆ Clean hanging chandeliers. If the chandelier has baubles, each one must be removed and soaked for a few minutes in a solution of $\frac{1}{2}$ cup rubbing alcohol and $\frac{1}{4}$ cup powdered dish washer detergent per gallon of water. Most lighting shops carry a spray that can be sprayed on the baubles without removing them; cover furniture with plastic and place towels on top to catch drips.

Quarterly chores are often easy to remember because every calendar—and not just your special cleaning calendar—has built-in reminders. Every time the season changes, you'll know it's time to knock out these tasks.

Yearly Yokes

Great things happen annually: end-of-the-year holidays, your birthday, your anniversary—and these special cleaning chores!

♦ Replace the filters in your forced-air heating system (actually, twice a year is better than once). This cuts down on allergic reactions, preserves the life of the motor and blower, and keeps the ductwork clean. Generally the filter is in the side of the heater that is located in the garage.

♦ Clean the lint out of your dryer vent. Lint does more than make your clothes look messy. It also builds up in your dryer vent, decreasing the dryer's efficiency and creating a fire hazard. Every six months to one year, detach the 4-inch duct that leads outside the house. If the hose is long, use a vent cleaning brush to clear out the lint; if the hose is short, simply reach in and pull out the lint, then use a rag to get at the last bits. You can also use a vacuum if the lint buildup isn't too severe.

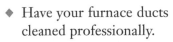 **Mary's Handy Hints**

A wet or dry vac works very, very well for cleaning dryer hoses. The extension tube usually reaches the entire length of the hose. After vacuuming the hose, cover a tennis ball with an old cotton tube sock and duct tape the sock and ball to the end of the extension tube. Run it down the hose to finish cleaning.

♦ Have your furnace ducts cleaned professionally.

♦ Check for mold in bathrooms and treat if needed. Contact a medical supply store for a 20 percent solution of hydrogen peroxide. Dilute 50/50 with water. Remove all towels and rugs. Spray the mold, wait 30 minutes and treat a second time. Then wait 24 hours and treat again if needed, using the peroxide full strength.

- Move all heavy furniture to clean behind and underneath it. Check for any unwanted critters. It's a good idea to spray under the bed for dust mites that love to hide there. Go to a garden store that sells organic fertilizers and pesticides. If you don't have such a store in your area, search the Internet for organic pesticides. Several organic gardening books also carry excellent home remedies for killing unwanted pests.

- Clean closets and donate anything you haven't worn in the past year. Remember that clothes you donate to charity are tax deductible, so get a receipt and place the slip in your tax records.

These tasks tend to be heavy duty compared with the daily and weekly chores, but because you have an entire year to recover from them, they shouldn't be too scary.

The Least You Need to Know

- Without schedules, the world—and your home—will turn into a seething mass of chaos.

- Come up with a cleaning schedule that works for both you and your family.

- Prevention is key! Daily tasks are those little things that keep your home running smoothly and make your bigger chores a bit less onerous.

- Schedule tasks on your calendar so you don't forget things that are easy to ignore, such as changing the filters in your forced-air heating system or dusting the ceilings for cobwebs.

Chapter **3**

Green and Clean

In This Chapter

◆ Deciding whether you should go green

◆ Green cleaning and your health

◆ Green cleaning and the environment

◆ Using green tools and recipes for a clean home

Kermit the Frog once sang, "It's not easy being green." Well, as much as we hate to argue with a puppet, we have to say that Kermit was wrong. Although going green in your home takes some effort, eventually you'll find that it's even easier than picking up a bottle of chemical-laden cleaning spray at the supermarket.

More and more people these days are choosing to use all-natural cleaning products as they learn more about the harmful environmental and health effects of the chemicals in many store-bought cleaning solutions.

Why Go Green?

You might like the idea of going green, but wonder about all the work involved. Why bother mixing up your own cleaning solutions like some mad scientist or making special trips to the health-food store for green products when you can buy something pre-made at the local supermarket that you know is going to work? Besides, you don't even know where to get things like 20 percent hydrogen peroxide and Nature's Miracle. Gimme some good old Formula 409 and Pledge any day, you say.

Don't be so hasty, friend. There are several good reasons for cleaning green, namely that doing so is good for your health, good for the environment, and—last but not least—good for your pocketbook.

Going Green for Good Health

Most homes are built with super-heavy insulation to provide barriers against cold and heat. Although these barriers are useful in terms of living comfortably, those same barriers prevent toxic chemicals from being vented outside the home, thus causing them to build up in your environment over time.

Where do these toxic chemicals come from? Chemical cleaning products that line the shelves of every supermarket from coast to coast. Anyone who's ever read a warning label on an oven cleaner, bathroom spray, deodorizer, or toilet bowl wash won't be surprised to learn how dangerous these products can be.

What might be surprising, though, is how these products can harm you even when used properly. Researchers are now linking a buildup of fumes and chemicals in the home to cancer, adult-onset asthma, and a multitude of other health issues.

Mary's Handy Hints

If you aren't "going green" in your home, see Chapter 12 for information on how to ventilate your home.

The problem lies with using a multitude of products. People may use up to five products to clean their home during a short period of time, and if a home is sealed to the outside—as many are thanks to central air—the fumes remain in the home for long periods of time.

Here are some popular commercial cleaning products and the effects they can have on your health. This list is partial; it would take a whole book to list the chemicals found in these products and their health effects!

- **All-purpose cleaners.** These cleaners are sprays that you spritz all over your kitchen and bathroom counters and scrubs that you use in your sinks and tubs. These products may contain morpho-line, which is a kidney and liver poison; sodium bromide, which can cause confusion; and neurotoxins such as naphtha, kerosene, Stoddard solvent, and glycol ether, which can cause confusion, headaches, and symptoms of mental illness. You read that right: symptoms of mental illness.

- **Deodorizers.** It's great to make your home and your things smell nice, but these products may contain chemicals that can cause allergic reactions, headaches, lack of concentration, confusion, symptoms of mental illness, and more. A chemical called methoxy-chlor accumulates in fat cells and can even turn up in a mother's breast milk. Studies show that animals exposed to high doses of methoxychlor experience tremors, convulsions, and seizures.

- **Dishwashing detergent (hand, not machine washing).** These products may contain naphtha, which, as mentioned, can cause confusion, headaches, and symptoms of mental ill-ness. Diethanolamine is a possible liver poison and is a caustic ingredient.

- **Oven cleaners.** Oven cleaners may be full of ether-type solvents that can contain impurities such as carcinogen benzene and that can cause respiratory problems. Lye is corrosive and poisonous—that's why you have to wear gloves when cleaning the oven. Other ingredients can cause confusion, headaches, and symptoms of mental illness.

- **Toilet bowl cleaners.** Many of the chemicals in commercial toilet bowl cleaners are toxic and corrosive. Others are kidney and liver poisons. They can also cause—guess what—confusion, headaches, and symptoms of mental illness.

Experts use the analogy of an empty barrel to illustrate the effects of pollutants on the body. Imagine that you're an empty barrel. Every time you eat, breathe, or absorb a pollutant, your barrel fills a little. When the barrel is full, you become sick. In other words, pollutants add up. The good news: when you get away from toxins, the barrel eventually empties again.

Dishing the Dirt

According to the EPA, indoor pollution causes thousands of cancer deaths and hundreds of thousands of respiratory health problems annually. The American Lung Association reports that occupational lung disease is the number-one work-related illness in the United States. And as many as 15 percent of all newly diagnosed adult-onset asthma cases stem from indoor dust and cleaning chemicals.

Green Cleaning for a Green Environment

The Earth is important—it's the only home planet we have. It would be a different story if we could all head to Mars or Jupiter. But would it really be a different story? We'd probably damage those planets, too. So let's take care of the one we have.

Part of that is being careful in choosing how we clean our homes. Cleaning products may have toxic chemicals that leach into our water, and the throwaway packaging they're stored in fills up our landfills.

Here are some of the effects the chemicals in our cleaning products can have on the environment. Again, this is not a complete list ... it would take ages to describe every chemical and its environmental effects!

- **All-purpose cleaners.** They clean your house, but dirty the environment. Petroleum distillates (naphtha), morpholine, and Stoddard solvent are considered hazardous waste. Chlorinated materials form other compounds that cause pollution and are stored in the fatty tissues of wildlife. Petroleum-based products are nonrenewable resources and can contain impurities that contaminate the water and air.

- **Deodorizers.** Having the air in your house smelling like wildflowers comes at an environmental cost. Deodorizers may contain salicylates, petroleum distillates, and other chemicals that are considered hazardous waste. Aromatic hydrocarbons (hydrocarbon is petroleum distillate, which is also called aliphatic hydrocarbon or mineral spirits) contain impurities that contaminate the water and air.

♦ **Dishwashing detergent (hand, not machine washing).** Complex phosphates can cause algae bloom. Other chemicals that may be in these products are considered hazardous waste. Chlorinated materials form other compounds that cause pollution and are stored in the fatty tissues of wildlife. Petroleum-based products are nonrenewable resources and can contain impurities that contaminate the water and air.

♦ **Oven cleaners.** Oven cleaners may contain yet more hazardous waste, including lye, petroleum distillates, and ether-type solvents. Chlorinated materials form other compounds that cause pollution and are stored in the fatty tissues of wildlife. Petroleum-based products are nonrenewable resources and can contain impurities that contaminate the water and air. (Sound familiar?)

♦ **Toilet bowl cleaners.** Just like the other products we listed, toilet bowl cleaners may contain chemicals that are considered hazardous waste, that pollute the water and air, and that are nonrenewable resources.

Just as you can picture your body as an empty barrel that gets filled with pollutants, you can imagine Earth as an enormous container slowly filling with toxic materials. The problem is there's nowhere to dump the barrel when it's full. We have to swim and walk in the environment we create, so the only real solution we have is to stop using these chemicals in the first place.

Dishing the Dirt

According to *Cleaning and Maintenance Magazine*, the janitorial sanitation industry is now turning to hydrogenated orange cleaners as a safe yet effective alternative to hazardous cleaning compounds. Considered to be a "green" product, hydrogenated orange cleaners, along with a few additional products, provide highly effective alternatives to these more harmful chemicals.

Going Green to Keep More Green

It sounds expensive to have to stock up on things such as 20 percent hydrogen peroxide and spray bottles, but going green really is cheaper in the long run than using commercial cleaning products. After all, you can buy a giant box of baking soda for just a buck or so. Many green laundry detergents recommend using a small amount, so the product lasts longer than its commercial counterparts. And things such as lemons are cheap—or even free if you're a gardener!

After you have all the ingredients you need on hand, you'll see that they last you a long time. Just a sprinkle of baking soda on your toilet brush will scrub a toilet. A third of a cup of vinegar in a bottle of water, and a squirt of a no-phosphate, natural dishwashing detergent are all it takes to make an all-purpose cleaner that lasts and lasts. And a container of salt will take forever to use up if you use it a sprinkle at a time.

Using Commercial Cleaning Products Safely

Even if you do decide to continue using commercial cleaning products, you can protect yourself with these tips:

- ◆ Open windows if you find you must use a strong detergent or paint. Leave them open for a period to air the room as effectively as possible. Ventilate the room with a fan.

- ◆ Never mix cleaning products together; doing so can create dangerous new chemicals.

- ◆ Spray only enough cleaner on the surface to clean, which reduces the amount of cleaner used. People mistakenly think that if a little is good, then a lot is even more effective. Give your product time to work rather than spraying additional cleanser. Spray and wait 20 to 30 minutes before cleaning.

- ◆ Purchase only fragrance-free cleaners and laundry detergents.

> **Cleaning Quips**
>
> "The best time for planning a book is while you're doing the dishes."
> —Agatha Christie

It sounds like a conspiracy theory ... Black helicopters are flying over your house at midnight! Aliens shot Kennedy! Your beloved house cleaning products are full of hazardous waste! But going green really can have a positive impact on your health and the environment.

Recipes for Green Cleaning

Now that we've scared the pants off you, here's the fun part: Recipes for eco-friendly and healthy cleaning solutions that you can make in your own home from (mostly) easy-to-find and inexpensive products.

Here's your shopping list:

- 1 gallon of white vinegar
- 1 bottle of rubbing alcohol
- 1 large box of baking soda
- 1 gallon distilled water
- Bi-O-Kleen, Bio Ox, or a concentrated orange cleaner without petroleum distillates or limonene (another harmful chemical)
- Nature's Miracle (an enzyme cleaner found at most pet stores)
- Foaming shaving cream
- 20 percent hydrogen peroxide (get this at medical supply stores)
- Lemons
- Salt
- Flour
- Borax
- Spray bottles (you can get these at the hardware store)
- Powder or salt shaker (to hold baking soda)
- Olive oil

Cheap enough for you? Some of these products may seem difficult to hunt down, but check your Yellow Pages and you may be surprised at what you can find.

Now, on to the recipes!

- ◆ **Floor cleaners.** Don't be concerned about disinfecting your kitchen floor. Your carpeting contains far more bacteria than a hard floor surface. Unless you disinfect your feet, disinfecting your floors serves no purpose and only ruins the sealants. The only exception is if you drop raw meat, an egg, milk, or other bacteria-laden food on the floor. Most hardwood floors and laminated floors can be cleaned with ¼ cup white vinegar per quart of water. Marble, tile, and granite floors can only be cleaned with very hot water. Cleaners of any kind will pit these floors. Linoleum floors are safely cleaned with just hot water. You can find more detailed information on cleaning floors in Chapter 9.

- ◆ **Scouring powder.** Sprinkle baking powder on the area to be scoured and scrub it with a damp sponge or cloth. You can even run the baking soda through the blender along with an aromatic herb or flower petals to give your scouring powder a pleasant smell.

Mary's Handy Hints _____

For even more information on going green, check out the book *Green and Clean* by Annie Berthold-Bond (Ceres Press, 1994).

- ◆ **Disinfecting cleaner.** Mix 1 cup of baking soda and ¼ cup borax. Put it in a bowl, scoop it up with a damp sponge, and scrub away. Alternatively, you can put the mixture into a shaker canister and shake it onto the surface to be disinfected.

- ◆ **Oven cleaner.** Mix concentrated orange cleaner and baking soda together into a paste. Scrape off what residue you can with a scouring pad, then scrub with the orange cleaner/baking soda mixture.

- ◆ **Air freshener.** To remove kitchen odors, boil a 50/50 solution of white vinegar to water for several minutes.

- ◆ **Mildew remover.** Mix a 50/50 solution of 20 percent hydrogen peroxide (found at medical supply stores) to water. Wipe or spray on the mildewed areas. After applying, wait 30 minutes and treat once again. Then wait one to two hours. If any mold remains on the surface, remove with a white cloth dipped in the peroxide mixture. No need to rinse. The peroxide will continue to kill any lingering mold.

- **Stubborn stain remover.** When all else fails, try foaming shaving cream. (Use only the foaming shaving cream; the gel doesn't work.) Spray it on the surface and resist the temptation to turn into a little kid again and smear it all over the place. Let it set 15 to 30 minutes, then rinse with ⅓ cup of white vinegar per quart of water. This works on carpet, clothing, fabric furniture, fabric shades, and other cloth items.

- **Drain opener.** Every month, pour 1 cup of baking soda down the tub, sink, and shower drains followed by 1 cup of white vinegar. (Do not do this on the side of your kitchen sink with the garbage disposal.) Substitute 1 cup of hydrogen peroxide for the vinegar if mold or mildew plague your drains. Wait two to three hours, and then flush with warm water.

Mary's Handy Hints

To help keep drains clog-free, switch soap. The talc in bar soap builds up not only on shower walls but also on the sides of the drains. The phosphate in liquid dish soap clogs up the kitchen drain. Switch to phosphate-free natural dish soaps and either glycerin, natural bar soap, or phosphate-free liquid body soap.

- **Window wash.** In a spray bottle, combine ¼ cup rubbing alcohol and ⅓ cup white vinegar, and fill with distilled water. You need to use distilled water for best results, because tap water can contain impurities that smear glass.

- **Toilet bowl cleaner.** Sprinkle baking soda around the inside of the toilet bowl. Pour in ⅓ cup of white vinegar. Scrub with a nylon toilet bowl brush. Once a month pour 1 cup of white vinegar into the toilet and leave overnight to prevent water rings.

- **Silver polish.** Put a sheet of aluminum foil into a plastic or glass bowl. Sprinkle the foil with salt and baking soda and fill the bowl with warm water. Soak your silver in the bowl. The tarnish migrates to the foil like magic! Dry and buff.

◆ **Crystal cleaner.** Try a mixture of vinegar, water, and a small amount of baking soda. Pour on a soft cloth and rub the crystal. Rinse with warm water and dry.

◆ **Brass.** Cut a lemon in half, sprinkle it with salt, and rub the lemon on the metal. Buff with a cloth.

◆ **Copper.** Make a paste with equal parts white vinegar, flour, and salt, leave on for an hour, then buff with a cloth. Copper also comes clean very well with tomato sauce … just rub in, let it sit for a bit, and rinse off.

Mary's Handy Hints

Make any liquid product that you create smell lemony fresh by adding ½ cup of lemon juice or a few drops of citrus essential oil.

◆ **Tub and shower cleaner.** Bi-O-Kleen, Bio Ox, and other orange cleaners that do not contain petroleum distillates do an excellent job cleaning bathroom showers and tubs and make a great all-purpose cleaner in the kitchen. Look for the concentrated cleaners to save money; they also clean better than the prediluted cleaners.

◆ **Bleach.** Switch to hydrogen peroxide, especially in the laundry. Bleach causes white clothes to turn dingy. A 50/50 solution of peroxide to water removes red wine stains and red dye food stains caused by pet food, punches, Kool-Aid, and popsicles. Soak shirts with yellow underarm stains in peroxide before laundering to remove those stains.

Cleaning Quips

"I got the blues thinking of the future, so I left off and made some marmalade. It's amazing how it cheers one up to shred oranges and scrub the floor."

—D. H. Lawrence

◆ **Furniture polish.** Mix a 50/50 solution of white vinegar and olive oil, spray on the surface, and wipe off with a clean cloth.

Eco-Friendly Products

Maybe you don't feel like spending time in the kitchen concocting your own cleaning products. That's understandable. But you can still go green by choosing to buy eco-friendly cleaning products. Here are just a few examples. You can check out your local health food store or supermarkets such as Whole Foods and Wild Oats for a wide array of green products. Also check out Appendix B for buying information.

- ◆ Bon Ami Cleaning Powder
- ◆ AURO All Purpose Cleaner
- ◆ Naturally Yours All Purpose Cleaner
- ◆ Ecover Dishwashing Liquid
- ◆ Life Tree Automatic Dishwashing Liquid
- ◆ Ecover Cream Scrub

The Least You Need to Know

- ◆ Going green is good for your health and the environment.
- ◆ Choosing to use eco-friendly products can save you money.
- ◆ You can go green with many products that you already have in your kitchen cupboards, such as salt, flour, and baking soda.
- ◆ Many of the products we suggest using in this book are green. If you prefer to use commercial products instead, you can—it's your decision!

Part 2

Cleaning House: A Room-by-Room Guide

A room's a room—whip out some all-purpose cleaner and a rag and start wiping away. Right? Not quite. Each room has its own challenges and unique cleaning needs—from the kitchen, where the threat of food poisoning lurks, to the living room, where different types of wood furniture require different types of cleaning methods. So put away that bottle of all-purpose cleaner and listen up: we tell you how to clean your way through every room of your home, and we tell you which tools and products to use on which cleaning jobs.

Chapter 4

Kitchen Cleanliness

In This Chapter

- ◆ Attacking the germs in your kitchen
- ◆ Scouring sinks, drains, and garbage disposals
- ◆ Cleaning the big stuff
- ◆ Dishing it out

"Build it and they will come." No truer words could ever be said about a kitchen. It doesn't matter if you build a cave, cabin, condo, or mansion, the kitchen stands alone as the central gathering point of a home. People congregate there to talk, cook, play games, and oh yeah—eat. Because the kitchen is full of food that goes into our mouths, doesn't it make sense to keep it clean?

In this chapter we tell you how to do just that, from the stove to the fridge. You'll also learn how to put the kibosh on germs on every kitchen surface!

What's Living in Your Kitchen?

We try to be lighthearted and amusing in this book, but in some cases, we have to get all serious on you. To wit: The Centers for Disease Control and Prevention estimates that 76 million Americans get sick, more than 300,000 are hospitalized, and 5,000 people die from food-borne illnesses each year. Most at risk are children, the elderly, people with compromised immune systems, and pregnant women.

At home, we lose the battle against viruses and bacteria by not washing our hands before touching food, not cooking food thoroughly enough, letting foods sit out at room temperature, and letting juices from raw meat contaminate other foods on counters and cutting boards. Here are some of the little bugs that may be living in your foods—and in your kitchen:

♦ Shigellosis lurks in milk and dairy products, poultry, and potato salad. Food becomes contaminated when a human carrier doesn't wash his or her hands and then handles food that's not thoroughly cooked. Organisms multiply in food left at room temperature. Symptoms include abdominal cramps, diarrhea, fever, sometimes vomiting, and blood, pus, or mucus in the stool. (We told you we had to get serious in this section!)

♦ Campylobacteriosis is a bacteria in poultry, cattle, and sheep that can contaminate the meat and milk of these animals (well, except chickens ... we generally don't milk them). The chief sources are raw poultry, meat, and un-pasteurized milk. Symptoms include diarrhea, abdominal cramping, fever, and sometimes bloody stools.

♦ Listeriosis is a bacteria that hides out in soft cheese, unpasteurized milk, imported seafood products, frozen cooked crab meat, cooked shrimp, and cooked surimi (imitation shellfish). The Listeria bacteria resist heat, salt, nitrite, and

> **Mary's Handy Hints**
>
> To learn more about food-borne illnesses and how to protect yourself and your family, check out these websites: Fight Bac!, www.fightbac.org; Centers for Disease Control and Prevention: Foodborne Illnesses, www.cdc.gov/health/foodill.htm; FoodSafety.gov, www.foodsafety.gov.

acidity better than many other microorganisms. They survive and grow at low temperatures. Symptoms include fever, headache, nausea, and vomiting.

Dozens of other disgusting life forms can be transferred from food, hands, or your kitchen counter and cutting boards, but we think you get the idea. Now that we've properly scared you, we'll tell you how to keep your kitchen so clean that little buggers like these have nowhere to hide.

Putting the Kibosh on Clutter

What's easier to clean: a nice, bare counter or one that's cluttered with appliances, knife racks, cookbooks, and doodads? If you said the latter, you're ready to be a cleaning queen (or king).

Store rarely used appliances in cabinets whenever possible, and opt for built-in appliances (such as an above-the-stove microwave) when you get new ones. This will keep clutter from getting in the way of your cleaning.

Scouring Sinks

Ah, the sink—it's probably the dirtiest place in the kitchen, seeing as how that's where all the dirty dishes go, that's where we refill the dog's water bowl, and that's where we pour old beverages such as the milk that's been in the fridge so long it may qualify as a biohazard. Follow these tips to keep everything sparkling and fresh.

Stainless Steel

Stainless-steel sinks tend to get spotty or rusty, but fortunately they're easy to care for with products you already have around the house (and that you would never have thought to use in the kitchen!).

To clean your stainless sink, you need nothing more than a handful of baking soda and a brush. Scrub, rinse, and, most important, dry. Drying the sink after every use helps prevent rust and water marks.

If stubborn water marks are bugging you, dampen a heavy-duty paper towel with white vinegar and cover the marks with them. Keep the towels damp for an hour, then scrub the stains away with baking soda. Rust marks got you down? Rub with a little lighter fluid on a cloth.

Dirty Words _____

> Lighter fluid makes a great rust remover, but be very careful—it's very flammable (which is why we use it to light things)!

We know you—it's not enough that your sink sparkle. It has to gleam! Wipe it down with a bit of baby oil on a cloth, and your gleam dream will come true.

You'd better sit down for this one: according to a microbiologist from the University of Arizona, there is more fecal matter in your kitchen sink than in your toilet. You should regularly clean your kitchen sink, no matter what the type, with a disinfectant cleaner. Let the cleaner sit for a few minutes, then wipe it off with paper towels. Also wash your hands in the bathroom instead of the kitchen, wash out pets' bowls in the tub or bathroom sink, and never bathe young'uns in the kitchen sink (unless you empty the water into the bathtub).

Another way to disinfect the sink is to fill it with a solution of 1 gallon of water to 1 cup of hydrogen peroxide or white vinegar. You can even throw your dishrags and sponges in there while you're at it, because those are hotspots for germs. Let the mixture sit for five minutes, then open the drain and let all that disinfecting goodness run down. Do this monthly.

Cast Iron and Porcelain

If you're one of those people who like to leave dishes in the sink until the last possible second, it's time to change your ways. These sinks stain easily, and the stains can be tricky to remove. If you need encouragement to put your dishes away quickly, get a cast-iron or porcelain sink. The time and effort it takes to remove stains from these sinks will get you putting the dishes away pronto!

Use a soft cloth to dry the sink after each use; otherwise the water spots will wink at you every morning—and they don't come out. Do *not* use microfiber to dry or clean any sink. Made from 80 to 85 percent polyester—in other words, plastic—they will eventually scratch the sealant off any surface.

Use abrasive cleaners sparingly and only to remove a stubborn stain. To remove most stains, mix a paste of hydrogen peroxide and baking soda, rub gently with a soft cloth, rinse, then dry. Never use steel wool, wire brushes, or abrasive sponge pads.

Mary's Handy Hints

Use rinse baskets and sink mats to protect porcelain and cast-iron sinks.

For general cleaning, squirt a bit of your liquid dishwashing detergent into the sink and clean with a soft cloth, rinse, then dry. Borax and a nylon scrub brush also do a good job cleaning cast-iron sinks when the sink needs that extra cleaning boost. Use borax sparingly, wiping it off with a clean cloth.

Vitreous China and Fireclay

As with a cast-iron sink, dry vitreous china and fireclay sinks after each use.

Liquid dishwashing detergents work well on a week-to-week basis. Squirt a bit into the sink and wipe with a clean, soft cloth. Occasionally use soft abrasive cleaners such as Barkeeper's Friend or Cameo to clean these sinks. Never use strong abrasive cleaners; they'll scratch and remove the finish.

Composite (Acrylic, Quartz, and Granite)

Do not set hot pans, dishes containing acidic food such as tomato sauce, or tea or coffee cups directly on these surfaces. They stain easily, and the acid can damage the surface, especially if it sets for any length of time. Clean frequently with a mild detergent. Try using whitening toothpaste to remove stains. If that doesn't work, dampen a heavy-duty paper towel with hydrogen peroxide and plaster it to the stain. Keep the towel damp with peroxide for an hour or longer. Scrub with baking soda, then rinse.

Corian

That hot tomato sauce sure was yummy, but your Corian sink won't agree—heat and acidic foods can ruin Corian surfaces. Always rinse dishes thoroughly before setting them in a Corian sink. Never place a cup with tea or coffee in these sinks, because they stain easily. Prevention is the key to making any cleaning chore easier—especially when it comes to Corian.

Remove stains by first soaking them with hydrogen peroxide as you do with composite sinks. Scrub with a bit of baking soda after the peroxide has set for 15 to 20 minutes.

If that doesn't zap the stain, then use a white scrub pad found in most hardware stores. Don't use any other color because they're more abrasive and will scratch. Dampen the pad with peroxide and gently scrub to remove the stain.

Mary's Handy Hints

Those sink stoppers and rubber mats can get pretty dirty. Put them in the dishwasher and they'll come out cleaned and sanitized.

No need to polish Corian. Most Corian, because it is not a natural stone, tends to have variations in the sealant: one area will be shiny whereas another will look a bit dull. Applying a polish to Corian only makes the shiny spots stand out more and the dull spots look more pronounced.

De-Gunking Drains

We take our drains for granted. We pour all sorts of stuff down them, then we scratch our heads and wonder why they clog up or smell all (as we said in the '80s) grody. Here are some ways to get rid of the ick and keep your drains free-flowing and clean:

♦ Pour a cup of salt and a cup of baking soda down the drain. Follow this up with a kettle of boiling water, then finish by flushing with hot water for five minutes. This will cut through any hardened grease like magic.

◆ Once a month, follow the instructions for homemade drain cleaner in Chapter 3. After watching in amazement how the combination creates a volcano of fuzz, cover the drain for a few minutes, and then flush for five minutes with cold water.

◆ Whenever you have any boiling water left over, such as when you make tea, pour it down the drain. This will keep congealed grease from building up in the drain. Add a bit of liquid dishwashing detergent for an even stronger degreaser.

Don't use the baking soda tricks on the side of the sink with the garbage disposal, because undissolved baking soda can jam up the blades. For the side of the sink that houses the disposal, use an enzyme product such as Nature's Miracle, which you can get at pet stores. Once a month, pour 2 cups of this liquid down the disposal before going to bed. The enzymes "eat" any food that's jamming up the disposal (yummy!).

Clean Garbage Disposals—Not an Oxymoron

Of course it's dirty—after all, what goes down the garbage disposal? That's right—garbage. Here are some tips for getting it sparkling:

◆ Toss a few ice cubes into the disposal while it's running. This will help scour the mechanism clean.

◆ To dispel odors, run lemon peels (or even a whole lemon) through the disposal with plenty of water. This works especially well when you toss the lemon peels in at the same time as some ice cubes.

◆ A sink brush or a curved bottle brush is a nifty, inexpensive device that will help you clean the garbage disposal (and the drain). It's a long brush with a bulb-shaped tip; see Appendix B to find out where you can get one. To freshen the disposal, dampen either brush with water then pour on a tablespoon of baking soda.

◆ A product called Disposer Care claims to foam away the grunge. See Appendix B for info on where to find this product.

There! Now your garbage disposal is so clean and fresh that you won't want to put your garbage in it anymore. May we suggest a nice bouquet of roses?

Applying Yourself to Your Appliances

Those things cost a bundle—remember how much you paid for that fancy fridge with the ice dispenser, and that self-cleaning oven? Some basic good care will help keep those pricy appliances running better and longer (and looking better, too).

Freeing Your Fridge and Freezer from Filth

The fridge and freezer are the center of the kitchen—the place that holds all the treats you like to eat. Because spills happen, cross-contamination of foods can occur, and bad smells can taint the flavor of milk and other foods. That's why you need to wash your fridge every week (ideally before you do your weekly marketing); here's how.

Toss out anything that's past its prime. Then set foods that aren't highly perishable on the counter, and gather the rest together as well as you can on a shelf or two. If you can remove drawers and shelves, wash them in hot, soapy water and dry. Put the shelves you've removed back into the fridge, move the perishable foods onto them, and then remove and wash the shelves the perishable foods once inhabited.

When you're done with the shelves and drawers, unplug the fridge and wipe down the inside using warm, soapy water with a few tablespoons of baking soda mixed in. You can also use a sponge or cloth moistened with white vinegar, which kills mildew and removes bad odors. Borax and water also work quite well. Work from top to bottom. Finally, wipe down all surfaces with plain warm water and wipe dry, then plug the fridge back in.

Mary's Handy Hints

Be sure to use warm, not hot water, to wash glass shelves; hot water can make them crack. Add ½ cup of white vinegar to the water to make the shelves sparkle.

For folks who are too busy to clean the entire fridge at one time, each evening as you prepare dinner and have food out of the fridge, clean the shelves on one side of the refrigerator, saving the opposite side for the following night. Clean the drawers on the third night, followed by the door shelves and walls the next night.

The technique for washing out the freezer is pretty much the same, although you don't need to do it every week. Toss out all iffy foods and move the rest to an ice chest or the fridge. Unplug the fridge, and wash the freezer the same way you did the refrigerator.

Keep your fridge and freezer from becoming a wasteland of wilted lettuce and galloping germs with these other hints:

- The fridge handle was named a "hot zone" by a microbiologist who studies such things, meaning that it's one of the most bacteria-laden places in the entire house. Use an all-purpose cleaner to de-gross the handle.

- The door seal on your refrigerator will last a long time if you keep it clean. Every two months, wipe it well with a cloth or sponge and warm, soapy water. Be sure to run your cloth or sponge under the seal as well to catch any crumbs or drips hiding there.

- Check the seal on your refrigerator every year. To do this, close the door on a dollar bill. If the bill falls out (or if it pulls out easily), the seal needs to be replaced. The seal is held in place by simple screws, which makes it an easy do-it-yourself project. Seals should be replaced every three to four years to keep the refrigerator running efficiently.

- If your fridge has a drip pan, empty and sanitize it frequently to keep molds and other yuckies from growing in there. Pull it out every week, wash it in hot, soapy water, and sanitize it in a solution of 1 teaspoon of bleach to 1 quart of water. Let it sit for five minutes, drain and rinse, let it dry, and put it back.

- You may need to vacuum your fridge's condenser to keep it from getting clogged up with dust or pet hair; refer to the appliance's user manual to find out how and how often to do it or follow the schedule in Chapter 2. A curved bottle brush will help you get at the deepest parts of the coils—you won't believe how much the vacuum misses! Just be careful not to snag any of the wires.

- Vacuum the grill weekly; occasionally remove it and scrub with hot soapy water, wipe dry, and replace. A 1½-inch paintbrush quickly whisks away the dust in the grill as well.

Mary's Handy Hints

If space is of the essence in your fridge, drop a charcoal briquette into the toe of an old pair of panty hose cut off at the knee. Attach a suction cup with a hook just under a middle shelf toward the back and hang the panty hose from the hook by poking the hook through the panty hose.

♦ Clean the outside of your fridge with a mild solution of detergent or baking soda and water.

♦ Remove odors by placing a small tub of charcoal (like the kind used in fish tanks or even regular charcoal briquettes) on the middle rack. You can also use a tub or open carton of baking soda.

Don't let your fridge be the hot zone of the house! Follow these tips and you'll have one less thing to worry about.

Washing the Dishwasher

Dishes not coming out clean? A common problem is that the water inlet valve has deteriorated from the chlorine in the water and fails to provide enough H_2O to clean the dishes. To check on this, start the machine, then open it once it's filled. There should be enough water on the bottom of the dishwasher to touch the sides. It there's just a small puddle of water, you need to replace the water inlet valve. This is a simple do-it-yourself job: the valve is at the front of the machine and there are only two wires, which can be interchanged.

If your dishwasher is emitting a funky smell, pour borax into the dispensers and run the washer without any dishes in it.

Mary's Handy Hints

To make cleaning easier, smart cooks (like yourself!) clean as they go. Make sure the dishwasher is empty so you can load in dishes as you dirty them. Keep the trash can out so you can toss in those potato peels and product packages. Wash a pan while you're waiting for the water to boil. This way, when you're done cooking, you'll have a minor mess to deal with instead of a major one.

Hot, Hot, Hot: Ovens and Stoves

If you're lucky, you have a self-cleaning oven—just lock the door, turn it on, and it's off to the races! Clean these ovens only according to the manufacturer's directions; if you try using regular oven cleaners inside self-cleaning ovens, you will wreck their self-cleaning surfaces. The same goes for continuous-cleaning ovens.

But if you aren't lucky enough to have a self-cleaning oven, you'll have to do it old-school style—and by that, we mean manually, just like the cavemen did. Get a professional-strength oven cleaner product from a janitorial supply store; spray it on the inside surfaces of the oven, leave on for 10 minutes, and wipe off. It works quickly with no harsh odor.

Be sure to open the window and have a fan running when cleaning the oven. Some chemicals may not have odors, but they're still there, and the room must be ventilated.

Want to clean sans chemicals? Make a paste of baking soda and orange-based cleaner. (Just make sure it doesn't contain petroleum distillates.) Paste it onto the oven's surfaces and let it sit for a couple of hours. Wipe, and repeat if needed. Finally, rinse with white vinegar and water, which will help remove the cleaner.

Always place plastic on the floor before using a chemical oven cleaner, because the cleaner will damage the floor. Wear protective gloves and old clothes.

Prevent messes in the oven and you won't have to clean it so often. Place baking sheets or a sheet of foil under casseroles that may bubble over. Use lids on baking dishes when possible. Use deep pans so splatters are contained.

 Mary's Handy Hints
Sprinkle salt on oven spills; the gunk will come right up once the oven is cool.

As for the cooktop, light messes can usually be cleaned up with nothing but detergent, water, and a little elbow grease (available at your local elbow grease store). Or wet a dish rag with really hot water, lay it over any baked-on spots, and go have dinner. When you get back to the kitchen, use the rag to wipe off the now-softened spots.

For more stubborn gook, try Bon Ami, which has a mild pumice action, or use a plastic scraper; see Appendix B for buying information. And believe it or not, nongel toothpaste, rubbed in with a cloth, can get rid of soiled spots. (It's great for your teeth, too!) Follow up all these treatments with a detergent-and-water wiping.

Have an electric stove? The drip pans do more than catch drips—they also reflect heat back up onto the skillet or pot. When the drip pans get dirty, they absorb heat instead of reflecting it, decreasing efficiency and causing other glitches. Replace the drip pans with shiny new ones every three years.

We've tried not to talk about it, but we can avoid it no longer—the underside of the stove hood. You know, the place that collects all sorts of grease and grime, but that we never clean because we can't see it unless we crane our necks.

Here's a tip that's so easy that you'll start looking forward to cleaning under the hood. (Okay, nothing is *that* easy.) Spray the underside of the hood with a foaming tub and tile cleaner. It's an excellent degreaser.

Dirty Words

Do not use abrasive pads or cleansers on your cooktop—they can scratch the surface.

It foams and the grease drips right down. Place some newspaper on top of the stove to catch the drips, and wipe with a clean but old terry towel. It cleans up in seconds! This tip works well with grease buildup on the outer parts of the stove hood, too.

Cleaning the Counters

Many counters can be cleaned with all-purpose cleaner. However, don't use all-purpose cleaner on granite, marble, or stone, or you may pit the surface. Instead, use a small amount of a liquid dish detergent that doesn't contain petroleum distillates, and dry thoroughly.

Neatening the Nuker

The microwave oven is a favorite place for grease and splatters to hide out. Check out the ceiling of your nuker—yep, that's from the bacon you cooked in there last week. And that stuff on the walls? We don't even know what that is.

Well, here's an easy way to get rid of all that. Wet a dish cloth, place it in the middle of the microwave, and microwave it for 30 to 40 seconds. Wait for the cloth to become cool enough to touch, and use it to wipe away all the mess that the steam has just helped to loosen.

Don't feel like cooking any dish rags today? Fill a coffee cup half full with water and microwave for three minutes. Let it rest for a minute, then wipe off the loosened grime with a towel.

Or forget all the fancy tips and simply clean up the inside of the microwave with detergent and water. To nix stubborn grease, let the detergent and water solution sit on it for a minute before wiping up. Still no go? Try a nylon mesh pad designed for nonstick cookware.

Cleaning the Coffeemaker

This is probably the most important appliance in your kitchen. After all, only a jolt of java can get you ready for the day. No java, no work. No work, no money. No money, no java. You see the problem. So we'll tell you how to take care of your coffeemaker.

Every few months, fill the water reservoir with white vinegar and let the coffeemaker run through its cycle. Do not drink the resulting liquid—we tried it, and although it's better than some cheaper brands of coffee, it's still pretty vile. Then clean out the pot and run fresh water through the coffeemaker. This will get rid of mineral deposits and other gunk.

To clean the filter basket and other removable parts, soak them in hot water with dishwashing detergent and ½ cup of white vinegar. (No, we do not hold stock in the white vinegar company.)

The coffee pot itself will come clean if you rub it with a paste of baking soda and water.

Mary's Handy Hints

Sick of using vinegar? You can buy coffee maker cleaner at specialty stores, which get will rid of the oils left from the coffee and mineral deposits from the water. Check kitchen stores or websites like www.chefsresource.com.

Dishing (Off) the Dirt

Don't have a dishwasher? Don't fret. Doing the dishes by hand is a great meditative practice. We're not kidding: an old Zen parable tells of a monk who asked his master how to reach enlightenment. The master asked, "Have you cleaned your rice bowl yet?" No, the monk replied. "Then you had better do it," the master said. At that, the monk was enlightened.

Although washing the dishes may not help you reach Nirvana, it will give you time to think and reflect—and most important, it will keep dirty dishes from taking over your kitchen. Read on for the 411 on how to clean dishes with confidence.

Move Fast

You should be cleaning as you cook, but there are always some last-minute items that you can't get to right away because, say, you have dinner waiting. Pour off grease or oil into a can (which you can put in the fridge to harden the grease before you chuck it into the trash), scrape away cooked-on food as best you can, and put the dishes in a sink full of hot, soapy water to soak. This will make your job much easier after dinner.

If food has burned onto a pot or pan, fill it with some water and simmer for 10 minutes as you eat dinner. Set the timer, then toss in any cooking utensils that need extra soaking.

Ready ...

To the right of the sink, stack dishes in the order in which they'll be washed:

1. Glasses

2. Flatware

3. Plates

4. Bowls

5. Serving dishes

6. Mixing bowls

7. Cooking utensils

8. Pots, pans, casseroles, and skillets

This may seem like some random order that we made up because we're on a weird dish-related power trip. But really, there is a good reason for the order: we're going from least soiled to most soiled so that the washing water stays clean as long as possible and doesn't need to be changed as often. Glasses and flatware also need to be washed in very hot water so they don't develop spots; taking care of them first lets them be washed when the water is at its hottest.

Set ...

To the left of the sink, you should have a clean dish-draining rack on a draining mat placed so that the water drains off into the sink.

Most people wash in the right side of the double sink and rinse on the left; perhaps this is because most people are right-handed. Or maybe it's merely another random, power-trippy rule we just made up. If you like, you can switch the sides. (Just don't tell us about it!) If you have a garbage disposal, wash your dishes in the side of the sink that houses the disposal to avoid gunking up your drains.

If you have no double sink, set a plastic or rubber dishpan on one side of the sink to hold soapy water, and use the other side of the sink for rinsing.

Make sure your dishwashing utensils of choice are sparkling clean; we tell you how to clean them later in this chapter. Some things you may want to use include the following:

♦ Dish rags

♦ Pot scratchers (nylon for nonstick pots and skillets, metal for cast iron)

♦ Bottle brushes

♦ Sponges

You should also have a good-quality dishwashing liquid that doesn't contain phosphorus, which can clog up your drains.

Go!

Fill the sink with very hot water—it should be so hot that it's uncomfortable to stick your hands in there for too long. (You can wear oh-so-fashionable rubber gloves if this bothers you.) Change the water whenever it becomes too dirty or oily, and run in more hot water if it becomes too cool.

Use as much dishwashing liquid as the directions on the label recommend; there should be enough that the dishes come clean easily, but not so much that it takes you five minutes to rinse off every item. You can use less if you add ⅓ cup of vinegar to boost the detergent's cleaning ability.

Wash similar items together to reduce the chance of breaking your beautiful glasses and dishes; for example, don't toss a cast-iron skillet on top of your stemware. Whatever washing utensil you use—dish cloth, brush, or whatever—you'll need to feel the dishes with your hands to make sure they're no longer oily and have no minuscule food remnants stuck on them.

> **Mary's Handy Hints**
>
> If two glasses get stuck together, fill the top one with cool water and set the bottom one in warm water for a few minutes, then gently separate them. Remember science class? The cool water makes the top glass contract, and the warm water makes the bottom glass expand.

To finish, mix a 50/50 solution of water and white vinegar in a spray bottle. When the dishes are finished, simply spray any remaining suds with the mixture. Vinegar breaks down the suds so you don't spend hours rinsing dishes or the sink. The same holds true for rinsing suds off anything.

Hand Drying vs. Air Drying: The Debate Rages On

Some cleaning experts believe that it's more sanitary to air dry dishes, as people tend to use not-so-fresh towels to do the drying, thereby spreading bacteria all over their nice, clean dishes. But if you use freshly laundered towels, and change them whenever they become damp or dirty, you should be fine. Besides, stainless steel and aluminum pots and pans tend to look streaky if they're not dried with a towel, and cast-iron pans can rust if left wet.

Minimal counter space generally rules out air drying dishes unless the home has only one or two people. Can you imagine the counter space a family of four would need?

Most people who hand wash their dishes set aside one towel to only dry dishes and use another for all other purposes.

Mary's Handy Hints

Use special linen towels called "glass towels" to dry china and glassware. Glass towels are soft and lint-free, and you can buy them at department stores or kitchen stores.

Coming Clean with Your Cabinets

Cabinets are probably the most expensive thing in your kitchen, yet no one ever tells you how to care for them. We're here to fix that.

Don't use microfiber cloths to clean cabinets and wood furniture; it scratches and will eventually strip the sealant or finish off any surface, including cabinets, floors, vehicles of any kind, or painted walls. Not exactly the results you were looking for.

Use only 100 percent cotton towels for cleaning cabinets. Sponges and dish cloths contain more grease and oil than you find in most kitchen sinks and counteract your good intentions. Dampen a cotton cloth in a sink of sudsy lukewarm water, clean the cabinets, always working with the direction of the grain, and then immediately dry them. Treat door pulls in the same manner. Because these areas are a haven for oily buildup, including oil from fingertips, they require extra attention to prevent the finish from deteriorating.

Clean cabinets located above the stove, below the sink, and all frequently used cabinets on a weekly basis. Dust all cabinets with a barely damp cloth monthly. Clean with the sudsy water four times a year unless you are cooking with a lot of oil and grease, in which case twice a month is a necessity.

Dirty Words _____

Spray wood cleaners and spray oils will build up on your cabinets and gum up the finish, which means you'll have to refinish your cabinets ... not a cheap or easy project!

Way back in the days of yore, cabinets came in one finish: wood. Now they come in tons of creative and beautiful finishes. That's the good news. The not-as-good news is that each finish requires a different treatment, and using the wrong one can ruin your big kitchen investment.

Whitewashed and Painted Cabinets

Whitewashed cabinets come labeled so from the factory. For either cabinet, clean with sudsy water and a soft cloth. Conditioners and wood treatments will not penetrate white wash or paint and can't be used to condition and protect either cabinet. Think twice before installing whitewashed cabinets or painting the ones you currently have in your kitchen. Wood naturally dries and must be conditioned to prevent it from cracking.

Acrylic

These finishes have been popular for several years in the RV industry and are now becoming more prevalent in the home. In short, the cabinet looks like it has 50 layers of a polyurethane finish on it. Acrylic-finished cabinets cannot be treated with a wood conditioner, but the wood won't dry or crack like whitewashed or painted cabinets. Use only 100 percent cotton towels to clean. Hand and cooking oil damage the finish, so these cabinets must be cleaned weekly—particularly around the door pulls—to prevent deterioration of the finish. Do not apply any kind of polish or wax.

Tung Oil and Baked Finishes

Baked finishes usually have a light glossy look, although not as heavy as acrylic. Most cabinet finishes are of this type. They should be dusted with a barely damp cotton cloth at least once a month (twice a month if you live in the desert or a highly dusty area). Clean around door pulls weekly with warm sudsy water.

Condition at least twice a year with wood conditioner or the wood may dry and crack. Do not use conditioners or treatments containing petroleum distillates. Distillates are unhealthy to breathe and can damage some cabinet as well as furniture finishes.

Veneer

Dust these frequently to prevent dust from settling in the veneer and drying it. Treat as you would for tung oil finishes. Veneer cabinets require conditioning at least twice a year to prevent drying and cracking, or three to four times a year if you live in a dry climate.

The Gross Stuff: Trash Cans, Dishrags, and Sponges

Okay, the part about what's in your sink was pretty gross, but here are some more yucky facts: damp, crumb-laden dishrags and sponges make cozy homes for bacteria. We blithely wipe them all over the kitchen, not knowing that we're spreading germs all over the place. After all, if we can't see them they're not there, right?

Then there's the trash can. The liner occasionally leaks, and mold and bacteria feast on the goo. Kids (and adults) often miss the liner, and food goes sliding down the outside.

Cleaning to the rescue! Here's how to put the kibosh on the yucky stuff.

Cleaning Quips

"Cleaning your house while your kids are still growing is like shoveling the walk before it stops snowing."

—Phyllis Diller

Garbage Cans

Kitchen trash cans need a good washing at least monthly. Take the can outside, turn the hose on it, toss in a ⅓ to ½ cup (depending on the size of the can) of borax or powdered laundry detergent, and scrub with a brush like a toilet bowl brush—only don't use the one you use for bathrooms.

Spray down the outside of the can well with an all-purpose cleaner or a foaming tub and tile cleaner. Let it sit for a minute or two to do its work, then wipe down.

Dishrags and Sponges

Dishrags must be clean, clean, clean. They're cheap and easy to launder, so why not buy a bunch? That way you can replace your dish cloth whenever it gets dirty.

Y'know all those holes in sponges? They make great hideaways for germs. To disinfect a sponge, wedge it into the dishwasher with the dishes and run it through a cycle, or zap the damp sponge in the microwave for a few seconds. (Make sure it's cool before taking it out!) Sponges are also cheap, so replace yours often.

The Least You Need to Know

- ◆ In terms of germs, your kitchen may be worse than your bathroom. Keep the kitchen as clean as possible to ward off food-borne illnesses.

- ◆ Many of the appliances in your kitchen can be cleaned with stuff you already have around the house, from baking soda to baby oil.

- ◆ They say prevention is the best medicine (who are "they," anyway?). Well, they're right. Cleaning as you cook and preventing spills from happening in the first place makes your cleaning job easier.

- ◆ Washing your dishes by hand is not only a good meditative practice—if you do it right, dishes will be squeaky clean.

Chapter 5

Bathroom Blitz

In This Chapter

- ◆ Eliminating germs in your bathroom
- ◆ Brushing the bowl
- ◆ Scrubbing the tub with a rub-a-dub-dub
- ◆ Cleaning grout and tile

We read stories in the newspaper about soldiers learning to protect themselves against germ warfare, and we shudder at the thought of finding ourselves in a similar situation—yet we face a low-intensity germ warfare of our own every time we enter the bathroom.

Yes, the bathroom, the most dreaded cleaning challenge in any home—soap scum, mold between the shower tiles, that nearly unreachable spot behind the base of the toilet, and, of course, the genesis of many of these germs—the porcelain pedestal itself.

No need to reach for a gas mask—the tips in this chapter lay out a battle plan that's easy to follow no matter what your combat experience. Put this plan into action and you'll soon have those germs waving little white flags.

Tiny Toilet Terrors

If you were to interview a bacterium and ask for its ideal vacation spot, you'd find that it's not too picky. "Oh, anyplace is good," it would say. "But the warmer and damper the location, the more I'll like it." Warm and damp? Sounds like the perfect description of a typical bathroom.

To prevent bacteria from multiplying (and eventually doing complicated quadratic equations), keep the bathroom ventilated and dry. Open the window after showering when possible, and hang towels and washcloths so they dry (which they won't if they're crumpled on the floor). Push the shower curtain open after showering so the shower stall will dry, then close the curtain so the water on it will evaporate.

Just as important is proper bathroom hygiene. Make sure you (and your family) wash your hands after using the toilet. Use warm, soapy water, and lather up for as long as it takes you to sing "Happy Birthday" twice. Tip: Do not sing out loud, especially if you are in a public restroom. Make sure to get under nails and under rings where germs may lurk. Using paper towels to dry your hands means any lingering germs go in the trash, and not on a communal towel.

Conquering Clutter

It sure is hard to clean a bathroom where every surface is overflowing with soaps, shampoos, makeup, cotton swabs, and other toiletries. Try stashing your toiletries on a shelving unit that straddles the toilet, in the drawers of the vanity, or in hanging baskets. In the bath, instead of using the window sill or edge of the tub as a storing place, use a shower caddy that hangs from the shower head. This will make your cleaning job much easier.

Get ready to be grossed out: every time you flush the toilet, a fine mist of whatever is in there (don't ask) sprays out and settles on surfaces such as the outside of the toilet, the sink, and (get ready for it) your toothbrush. In 1975, Professor Charles Gerba of the University of Arizona published a scientific article describing the phenomenon of bacterial and viral aerosols due to toilet flushing. According to Gerba, close-up photos of the germy acrosol look like "Baghdad at night during a U.S. air attack." The moral of the story: *always* close the lid before flushing!

Cleaning the Toilet

Okay, despite the picture we painted in the introduction, the toilet really isn't a land mine of germs. In fact, in studies by Professor Charles Gerba of the University of Arizona, the toilet seat was the least contaminated area of 15 household locales studied. Does this mean you should start using toilet seats as TV trays for snacks and drinks? No, it does not. "Least contaminated" is still contaminated, after all, so let's learn how to beat back the bacteria.

Weekly Toilet Tidying

Sprinkle baking soda around the inside of the toilet bowl. Pour in ⅓ cup of white vinegar. Scrub with a nylon toilet bowl brush. Try keeping the baking soda in a clean parmesan cheese container with holes in the lid for easier sprinkling. Make sure to scrub the inside of the toilet and around the rim.

Spray down the outside of the toilet weekly with the 50/50 vinegar and water solution, and wipe dry with paper towels. If you have young kids who sometimes can't manage to hit the mark, you can use this solution to deodorize and disinfect, so keep a bottle handy in the bathroom. You can store a bottle safely without fear of your children accidentally drinking the "cleaner."

Mary's Handy Hints

For "accidents" around the toilet, you can clean any type of flooring with Nature's Miracle, an enzyme product that you can find at the pet store.

One Ring to Rule the Bowl

Ring around the toilet! Ring around the toilet! Don't let your toilet be mocked like the people in the old Whisk commercial. Back the water out of the bowl by putting on a rubber glove and plunging your hand down the opening a couple of times, then grab a product called Erase It for Bathrooms. Customers who use this product have reported to us that it's removed rings nothing else could budge.

Work your way around the ring with the Erase It. Alternately, if you can't or don't want to use the Erase It, you can use a pumice stone. Be very, very careful using this stone because it will scratch your bowl.

> **Cleaning Quips**
>
> "The Rose Bowl is the only bowl I've ever seen that I didn't have to clean."
>
> —Erma Bombeck

Back the water out of your toilet, then dampen the stone with water and gently (gently!) work a small area until some of the stone appears on the toilet. Switch to a janitorial toothbrush or a white scrubbie pad and finish cleaning the bowl.

Potty Prevention

Spray a product called Advantage or your car wax—yes, car wax—on the inside of the rinsed and dried bowl and wipe to apply evenly. Let that dry for 10 to 15 minutes, wipe, then refill the bowl. Advantage and car waxes (such as 303 and Maguires) are both good because they contain substances that make a surface slick. We'll leave it to your imagination as to the benefits of a slick toilet bowl. Talk about prevention and easy cleaning!

For even more prevention, once a month pour a cup of white vinegar into your toilet bowl and leave it overnight. The mild acid in the vinegar neutralizes the alkali in the water, preventing rings from forming. How often you need to treat your toilets depends on the hardness of your water. If monthly treatment isn't working, then step it up to twice a month.

When you leave to go out of town for an extended period, pour a cup of (guess what?) white vinegar in the toilet. Then cover the bowl with plastic wrap. The plastic wrap prevents air from evaporating the water so you don't come home to water ring marks or ugly toilets. That way you can spend the month in Paris without worrying about your toilet!

Once every three months, pour a of couple cups of 3 percent hydrogen peroxide in the toilet tank. This keeps mold and mildew from building up in there, especially in an area that has high humidity. Let it sit overnight, then flush.

Rust Remover

If rust is coming down through the little holes in the toilet bowl, you need to clean the inside of the tank. Shut the valve and flush to drain, then go into the tank with a strong concentrated orange cleaner. Dilute the cleaner 50/50 with water and spray it on the sides of the tank, then scrub the tank with Bon Ami or Barkeeper's Friend.

As for the rust stains in the bowl, time to get out the Erase It for Bathrooms once again. It'll get those stains right out.

Scouring the Sink

Believe it or not, the place in the bathroom that harbors the most germs isn't the toilet—it's the sink drain! As we suggested for the kitchen sink in Chapter 4, every month you should toss a bunch of baking soda down the drain and top it off with white vinegar. The resulting fizzing action will scour out the drain and eat its way through any soap scum or other gunk.

On a weekly basis, clean the sink with diluted all-purpose cleaner such as Bi-O-Kleen, Orange Clean, or Bio Ox. Scrub out the little drain hole at the top of the basin with a toothbrush.

To clean soap scum from the sink, wipe it out with the all-purpose cleaner, undiluted. To get rid of that hard water ring around the drain, plug the drain and pour ½ cup of white vinegar into the sink. Let it sit all day, release the drain, then scrub the stain out with a toothbrush and baking soda.

Squeaky Clean Showers

If you like to sing in the shower, you may hit a sour note if your shower walls and glass doors are covered with water spots and soap scum. Get back in tune by following these tips.

Fiberglass Shower Stalls and Glass Doors

Alkalinity in the water causes those not-so-pretty spots on your glass doors and shower walls. To spite those spots, twice yearly, apply a car wax to the walls and doors. Both fiberglass and glass are porous, and the car wax seals those pores, which keeps water spots away and makes cleaning easier. Water sheets down rather than hanging on to the walls and door to leave its ugly marks behind.

Two tips on waxing the shower: first, make sure the wax doesn't contain petroleum distillates, which can be harmful to your health. Advantage is a good choice. Second, be sure to avoid getting wax on the floor unless you're a fan of extreme showering.

> **Mary's Handy Hints**
>
> If you're tired of fighting the battle of the soap scum, switch to liquid soap, natural soap, or Dove. It's the talc in most bar soaps that causes the buildup, so taking up a talcless soap will eliminate the scum. You'll still need to clean the shower once a week, but the job will be easier.

Squeegeeing or wiping down your shower after each use will help prevent soap scum and dirt buildup. Head down to an automotive store to purchase the California Squeegee made by the California Car Duster company. It's larger than bathroom squeegees, so it dries your showers faster.

You should clean the showers once a week with an orange citrus-based cleaner. Spray it on and give it 10 minutes to dissolve the dirt before wiping it off. Why do all that scrubbing when the product does it for you?

Okay, so the soap scum refuses to budge and the Queen of England is coming for a visit. Bring out both barrels: use your orange-based cleaner in its concentrated form. Pour plenty on an old dishrag and wipe on the walls and doors.

Patience now becomes a virtue. Wait and wait and wait some more. Go clean the rest of the house. Have a cup of coffee and read a novel. If the cleaner starts dripping down the walls, wipe it back on. Every so often, check the walls with a fingernail. If the residue removes easily, round one is almost over.

Use a white pad such as a Scotch-Brite pad to scrub. (Use the white ones only. The colored scrubbers are courser and do scratch.) Test a spot to make sure it won't scratch the fiberglass. Dampen the pad, keeping it good and wet, and gently scrub. This removes the soap buildup and most of the white mineral deposits on the glass doors. Nothing removes the etch marks themselves, but further damage is halted. Reapply the orange citrus cleaner if necessary.

Dirty Words

If you're using those daily bathroom sprays, you are breathing in their toxic fumes with each use and they're expensive. The buildup of chemical fumes in your home has now been linked to cancer, emphysema, and a host of other ailments.

The Tub

You don't need those chemical-laden tub sprays to clean your tub—after all, who wants to take a bath in a chemical residue soup? Try this instead:

1. Mix ⅛ cup of mild laundry detergent with 2 quarts of water and pour it into a spray bottle. Shake.

2. Start at the bottom of the tub, spraying the cleaner to the top.

3. Let the cleaner set a few minutes.

4. Scrub with a damp rag sprinkled with baking soda.

Now light some candles, pour a cup of tea, and take a nice, hot bath.

Ceramic Tiles

The big debate: some experts claim that acids (such as our beloved white vinegar) will etch ceramic tile and corrode grout. But others believe that a half-and-half solution of vinegar is much too mild to harm today's hardy ceramic finishes. We suggest using it only occasionally just to be safe.

Here's an easy homemade ceramic tile cleaner that will get your tiles all sparkly without acid and without harmful chemicals.

1. Mix ⅛ cup of mild laundry detergent with 2 quarts of water and pour it into a spray bottle.

2. Shake (the bottle, not yourself).

3. Spray the solution over your tub and tiles.

4. Use a sponge to wipe the solution (and dirt) from the tub and walls. White scrub pads also do a great job on bathroom tiles. Be sure to dampen them first with the cleaning solution.

5. Wipe dry with a terry towel.

It's so easy and cheap, you'll never want to use that foaming cleanser in your tub again!

De-Griming Grout

Then there's that stuff between the tiles—the grout. Y'know, that stuff that tends to turn grey with mildew at an infuriatingly fast pace.

To clean dirty grout, try a product called The StainEraser, which is a flat bar created specifically for removing mold and mildew from grout.

Grout is super porous, so mold and mildew can really get in there—and when they crash your pad, they throw rowdy parties and invite all their friends. If The StainEraser doesn't work (or you don't have one), first spray the grout with a foaming tub and tile cleaner (or the homemade solution in the previous section). The foamy goodness lets it stick to vertical surfaces, which is what you want. Let it sit for a while, then go at it with a toothbrush.

Next, spray the grout with a solution of half water and half 20 percent hydrogen peroxide, which you can get at medical supply stores. Wait half an hour to 45 minutes, then spray it again. Let this sit on the grout the whole day so it gets deep into the grout to kill off the mold and mildew.

The best thing you can do after you've killed the mold and mildew is to seal the grout. Go to a hardware store and get a five-year grout sealer with a sponge applicator, which makes it easier to use on a vertical surface. Put on quite a bit, let it dry for the amount of time recommended on the label, and then apply a second coat. Congratulations! You have finally won the war against grout mold and mildew.

Mary's Handy Hints

Prevention is key: take shorter, cooler showers. Steam causes cabinet doors to warp, wrecks paint, and lets mold and mildew thrive. Another suggestion: if your shower curtain is long enough, cut off the seam at the bottom to prevent mildew buildup down there. Take that!

Shower Curtains

Plastic shower curtains are great because they're waterproof and can be used to protect a prettier cloth curtain. They're not great because they tend to get that orangey mildew, with bonus black mildew on the bottom seam.

Thankfully, plastic shower curtains can be machine washed. Remove, spray with your diluted orange-based cleaner, and wait about 10 minutes. Wash it with your rags (the rags provide scrubbing action), and it comes out so clean you'll want to hang it in your living room instead of your bathroom. Air dry.

Faucets and Showerheads

Most faucets and showerheads are made from chrome, which you can clean with any nonabrasive cleaner. Clean, rinse, and dry to create a nice shine. You can remove stubborn water spots and rust with a solution of half water and half vinegar. If your faucets or showerhead aren't chrome, follow the manufacturer's directions for cleaning them.

Occasionally, remove your showerheads and soak them overnight in white vinegar to remove the buildup and dirt that clogs the holes. If you can't remove the showerhead, fasten a plastic bag full of vinegar around the showerhead with a rubber band.

If you have satin chrome, plated brass, or enamel faucets, you must dry them every time you use them or clean them to prevent discoloration.

The Fluffy Stuff: Bath Mats and Towels

How often do you clean your bath mat? We thought so. True, you only step on it with clean feet, but the fact that it tends to stay damp and warm means it can harbor bacteria. Wash yours regularly—once a month—according to the manufacturer's directions. Most bath mats with nonslip backing have to be washed in cold water and air dried, otherwise the backing will dry and crumble. Add ½ cup of white vinegar to the wash water to help disinfect.

Dirty Words

Do not use rubber-backed mats on linoleum or hardwood floors—they will leave yellow stains on the floor that you can never, ever remove. Use a light-colored cotton rug and nonslip pads, which don't stain the floor.

Change towels often to keep them from getting musty. (Who wants to rub a musty towel on their clean body?) Wash towels, only two or three at a time to avoid overcrowding, in warm water. Add ½ cup white vinegar to the rinse water to remove soap residue.

Cleaning the Trash Can

The bathroom trash can is a great place for germs to hang out, so wash it at least once every three to four months, or more often if it gets dirty. Add some hot water. Pour in a couple tablespoons of laundry detergent—it's low sudsing and easier to rinse. For extra cleaning power, add a few tablespoons of borax. Let it soak outside for an hour, scrub with a scrub brush, and rinse. Air dry upside down.

Mary's Handy Hints

Trash can liners will keep your trash cans from becoming filthy. Just lift 'em out and throw 'em away!

Creating Good Reflections on Your Mirrors

In a spray bottle, combine ¼ cup rubbing alcohol and ⅓ cup white vinegar, and fill with distilled water. (You need to use distilled water for best results, because tap water can contain impurities that smear glass.) Spray lightly onto the mirror and wipe dry in horizontal strokes with a clean, lint-free cloth.

De-Filthing the Floor

We're almost done with the bathroom, the bacteria are battle weary and looking for reinforcements, but there's nowhere left to hide—nowhere, that is, except the place that's easiest to overlook: the floor.

Don't think you can just stomp up and down on the little critters; they're a bit hardier than that. No, you need to marshal your forces for one final assault. Check out Chapter 9 for the scoop on cleaning floors.

The Least You Need to Know

- Bathroom hygiene is as important as cleaning when it comes to protecting yourself and your family from illness.

- Dampness is a bathroom's worst enemy—it causes mold and mildew, warped cabinets, and funky smells. Be sure to keep the place well ventilated.

- Who needs bleach? You can clean much of the bathroom using products such as vinegar, baking soda, hydrogen peroxide, and orange cleaner.

- Prevention is key! Wiping down the shower after each use will prevent mildew and water spots, sealing grout will prevent mold and mildew, and doing weekly cleaning will prevent big messes later on.

Chapter 6

Beautiful Bedrooms

In This Chapter

- ◆ Eighty-sixing clutter
- ◆ Maintaining your mattress
- ◆ Making a case for pillow cleanliness
- ◆ Clearing the closet

We spend at least a third of our lives—no, not at work, though it may feel that way—but in the bedroom. We sleep there, get dressed and undressed there. We read in bed and sometimes watch TV. When we're sick, the bedroom is where we recuperate. On special occasions, we even eat breakfast in bed.

Seeing as how we spend so much time and do so many things in the bedroom, it makes sense to keep it clean and comfortable. True, you could just close the door when you leave; no one will be able to see the mess. But who wants to retire at night to a room that's full of clutter and dust bunnies the size of actual bunnies, or to a bed that's covered with not-so-fresh linens? Not us!

Read on to find out how to create a clean, calming haven that's conducive to refreshing sleep.

Clearing Clutter

Once again, it's hard to keep a room clean if you're always tripping over books, trying to dust around toys, and vacuuming up discarded socks. Try finding a place for everything, and making sure everything's in its place. For example:

- Trunks make great storage for toys, books, and other items. Throw a cushion on top and you have seating that doubles as storage!

- Install a hook in the inside of your closet door to hang your robe in the morning.

- Plastic storage bins that can be stowed under the bed are a great place for storing away blankets and out-of-season clothes.

- Look into closet organizers, which will help you keep all your bedroom belongings stowed neatly away in the closet.

And this isn't all ... devise a system in your bedroom that works best for you with the creative use of shelving, hooks, storage boxes, hatboxes (for a pretty effect), and sets of drawers.

Maintaining Your Mattress

We can't do much about your partner hogging the mattress (and stealing the covers), but we can make sure that your mattress stays clean and fresh and gives you years of sleeping pleasure:

- Use a protective mattress cover to put the kibosh on stains.

- Never use dry-cleaning fluid on your mattress, because this can ruin the fabric or the underlying materials; it can also catch on fire if someone smokes in the bed! See Appendix A for information on how to clean various stains from your mattress.

- Turn your mattress every two weeks for the first three months, then once every two months; this keeps the materials inside the mattress evenly distributed so you don't get body dents so deep that you end up rolling off the bed (or into the center). To do this, you want to flip the mattress end to end *and* turn it over.

- Use a sturdy frame that has adequate center support so the mattress won't bow in the middle.

- If your mattress is more than 10 years old, it may be time to part ways and start fresh.

If it's time to say goodbye to your mattress, you can either ask the store where you're buying your new sleep set to pick up the old one, or call your local sanitation department. They usually have provisions for picking up large items, although you may have to make arrangements in advance. Goodwill or St. Vincent DePaul may also pick it up for you, giving you a tax deduction for the item to boot!

Follow these tips and you'll be sleeping soundly (although we can't help you with your partner's snoring problem).

Pillow Talk

Your pillow is one of the most important factors that decides whether you'll cut some good Zs or toss and turn all night, press the snooze button on your alarm clock a dozen times, get to work late, and get canned.

Mary's Handy Hints

If you rip off that mattress tag, the mattress police won't come after you—but the info on the label serves as a means of identification in case you have a warranty claim. If you remove it, you may not be able to return the mattress or have any defects solved.

Mary's Handy Hints

If you can, test pillows at the store by heading over to the bedding department with them and making yourself comfy on a mattress with your pillow picks. Or if you're sleeping at a friend's house and you find the pillow particularly refreshing, find out what the model and manufacturer are and try to find the same online or at a department store.

With the wide range of pillows competing for shelf (and bed) space, there's no excuse for sleeping on a subpar one. You can choose from body pillows, neck pillows, or head pillows filled with foam, feathers, buckwheat hulls, latex, and more.

Or pick a pillow for your particular pain. Got TMJ? There's a pillow for it. Do you snore like a buzz saw? A special pillow with a firm neck roll will let your significant other sleep in peace.

Pillow Woes: Wheezing and Sneezing

You wake up every morning exhausted, achy, and sneezing. You won't find the culprit under your nose—but under your head instead.

Finding a pillow can be a real ordeal, with all the choices out there. You've done your research and found that a goose down pillow is the right choice for your body, sleeping style, and wallet size—but soon your morning pain is replaced with a runny nose and itchy eyes. Now what?

A common cause of allergy woes is what's living in your pillow: dust mites. Dust mites are microscopic arachnids that feed on shed human skin. We're allergic to the excreted products dust mites produce. As we inhale them, our membranes respond and we get congested. Dust mites might be nearly invisible, but they're not invincible. They can't live in dry environments, so using a dehumidifier and an air conditioner to filter the air may reduce the number of mites that call your pillow home.

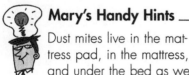

Mary's Handy Hints

Dust mites live in the mattress pad, in the mattress, and under the bed as well as in your pillows. You need to clean your mattress pad once a month and vacuum under the bed at least that often (weekly if you're allergic to dust mites). If you do have allergies to mites, cover the mattress with a plastic cover.

If you prefer not to deal with dehumidifiers—and the bathroom habits of tiny bugs—many stores carry nonallergenic fiber-fill pillows that have a special covering to prevent allergens from getting into or out of the pillow.

Keeping Your Pillow Pure

After you've discovered the best pillow, it's simply a matter of taking good care of it to ensure that the shape you fell in love with doesn't end up dirty and squashed beyond recognition. Follow these tips for keeping your pillow clean:

♦ **Buckwheat hull pillows.** When purchasing buckwheat pillows, make sure the label says they're "99% clean," otherwise the hulls may contain excess dust, which can cause sinus problems. Never wash or dampen buckwheat hulls; remove them to launder the zippered case. Place your buckwheat pillows in the freezer to kill any mites or other crawly creatures that might drop in for a visit. After one to two years you may need to add additional buckwheat as the buckwheat "polishes" down just a bit with use. Generally once is all that will be necessary.

Dirty Words

Never put even a barely damp pillow back into the pillow case. It will mold and mildew, then end up as another discarded item in the landfill.

♦ **Down pillows.** Machine wash your down pillow on the gentle cycle using mild detergent such as Woolite (not soap, which may leave residue). Don't use bleach, fabric softener, or a whitening detergent. Let the machine run for a bit to thoroughly mix the detergent and the water. Then stop the machine, push the pillows under the water, and squeeze out as much air as you can. Soak the pillows for about two hours, then squeeze out the air again. (If you have a pre-soak cycle on your machine, you can use that instead.)

Here's an expert secret: add a tennis ball or clean sneaker to the washer to keep the down from bunching up in a corner during the spin cycle. Restart the machine and complete the washing cycle. Add ¼ cup of white vinegar to the rinse water to deep-six detergent residue.

You can also hand wash your pillows in the tub using Woolite and rinsing with a tub full of water plus ½ cup of white vinegar.

Dry the pillows in the dryer on a low setting, removing them from the dryer frequently to refluff them with your hands.

◆ **Foam pillows.** Hand wash foam pillows in the tub using Woolite or a mild detergent. Keep pressing on the pillow to work the soap into the pillow, then let it soak for 30 minutes. Rinse by adding ½ cup of white vinegar to the rinse water. Again, press the water into the pillow to remove the soap. Air dry in the garage or basement. Never dry foam pillows in the sun or the dryer even on air dry. A foam pillow will catch on fire even on low heat.

◆ **Polyester pillows.** Unless you have a front-loading washer, it's best to take these pillows to a Laundromat and wash them in a large-capacity washer; they're too bulky for top-loading washers and can damage the washer. Use a mild detergent, such as Woolite, that does not contain bleach or a whitening agent. Use ¼ cup of white vinegar in the rinse to remove detergent residue. Machine dry on low heat.

◆ **Wool pillows.** Dry clean only. Of course, if your pillow comes with washing instructions, follow those. And whatever type of pillow you choose, invest in zippered pillow protectors that go on underneath the pillow case.

Making the Bed

Believe it or not, sheets and pillow cases do more than keep you comfy—they also protect your bedding and keep it clean. For example, the bottom sheet is comfortable, but it also protects your mattress, which isn't quite as easy to clean as a sheet. The top sheet keeps you warm, but it also protects the blanket above from skin oils and dirt. Again, it's easier to clean a sheet than a comforter or blanket.

That's why you want to keep your bedding clean. Be sure to launder and change it at least once a week. Every morning, you should also air out your bed while you shower and get ready for the day (because we lose an awful lot of fluids in our sleep, and they end up in the bed—how appetizing!).

Then it's time to make the bed. As we mentioned, you could leave your bed a crumpled mess and simply shut the door, but that means that at night, when you're tired and dragged out from a day of work and play, you'll open the door to find a messy bed instead of a clean sleep haven.

For those of us who have adopted the closed door policy, here's how to make a bed, starting from scratch:

- **Fit it.** Put on the bottom, fitted sheet. You may find it easier to start with the top corners.

- **Top it.** Place the top sheet on top of the fitted sheet with the wide hem toward the head of the bed and the narrow hem toward the foot of the bed. Tuck it in on all sides; if you want to be a stickler for detail (or if you're in the Army), create mitered or "hospital" corners.

- **Blanket it.** If you're using a blanket, place it over the bed and tuck it in all around, creating mitered corners if you like. Fold the top of the top sheet over the blanket; this protects the blanket as you sleep.

- **Be comfy.** Toss the comforter or duvet on the bed (leaving it untucked).

- **Finish it.** Finally, arrange your pillows in any way that makes you happy. You probably want to place any pillows with attractive shams in front of those that are merely covered with pillow cases.

After you learn to do this, it will take you just a few minutes every day. It's worth it to slip in between clean, unrumpled sheets every night!

Mary's Handy Hints _____

To create mitered corners, first tuck in the bottom edge of the sheet. Pick up the corner of the sheet and bring it around to the side of the bed. Put the side of the sheet up out of your way on the bed. Tuck in the part of the sheet that's left hanging down, then let the corner fall and tuck in the side of the sheet near the foot of the bed. Done! A bed any Army sergeant would be proud of. (Can you bounce a quarter off of it? Even better!)

Cleaning the Closet

If you're afraid to open the bedroom closet lest you be buried underneath an avalanche of clothes and shoes, it's time to take action. Follow these steps for creating a closet that works for you:

1. **Clear it out.** Take out all the clothes in your closet and place them on the bed. Take any other items from the closet and put them in a big box.

   Remember: If you haven't worn it in a year, it's time to say goodbye. It's hard to part with unflattering clothing that was given to you as a gift, so we're giving you permission here to toss the clothes—and the guilt.

2. **Sort it.** Sort your belongings into three piles: To Keep, To Give Away, and To Toss.

3. **Suck it up.** Vacuum out the closet and wipe down the walls and shelves with a barely damp cloth.

4. **Banish mold and mildew.** If the closet smells musty, find the source of the mold or mildew and treat it—otherwise your clothes will also smell musty. These bugaboos can also exacerbate your allergies!

5. **Get floored.** Clean the floors according to the instructions in Chapter 8.

6. **Put it back.** Put the clothing back, arranging it according to type of clothing and how often you wear it. For example, put all slacks together and all shirts together. If you wear track suits more than business suits, put the track suits near the front and the business suits farther back.

> **Mary's Handy Hints**
>
> Store shoes on a shoe rack. Some experts recommend stowing them away in boxes, but they need air in order to dry completely.

Now you can rest easy knowing that the items you need are in easy reach, and not lost in a chaotic jumble of clothes, hangers, and other stuff!

The Least You Need to Know

◆ Clearing the clutter will make your cleaning job easier.

◆ Use clever storage options to keep things such as books and kids' toys tucked away.

◆ A clean pillow will help you sleep better and put the kibosh on some allergies.

◆ Making the bed every day may seem like a pain, but it's worth it!

◆ When cleaning out the closet, be ruthless. If you haven't worn it in a year or more, toss it or give it away.

Chapter 7

Lovely Living Rooms

In This Chapter

- Giving the furniture some shine
- Taking care of the upholstery
- Knowing when it's curtains for you!
- Cleaning your knickknacks, lampshades, paintings, and more

The living room is, as the name suggests, where much of our living gets done. This includes reading, playing games, snacking, knitting, and watching TV (and some of us *do* live in front of the TV!). It's also usually the first place visitors see when they enter your home. It's like some crazy paradox: you do everything in this room, and yet you want to keep it clean, so it looks as if you *don't* do everything in this room. This chapter will help you straighten out (and straighten up) this crazy paradox, so read on.

De-Cluttering the Living Room

We mentioned that we gather in the living room to read, visit, watch TV, and do hobbies. And what do those things mean?

Books, magazines, newspapers, coffee cups, TV remotes, knitting needles ... you get the picture.

Your mom always said, "A place for everything, and everything in its place." And you know what? She was right. Snag a cheap basket to hold your remotes and another for your hobby items, a small bookshelf for books, a magazine rack for (guess what?) magazines. Place knickknacks behind glass so they don't accumulate dust.

Getting rid of the clutter will make it easier to keep things clean. After all, it's no small task to polish the furniture if you have to first clear it of junk, figurines, and other small items out in the open that collect dust.

Polishing the Furniture

Wax on, wax off. It may have been that simple for Mr. Miyagi, but it's not that simple when we're talking about polishing wood furniture. Before you wax on *or* wax off, you need to determine whether your furniture has a hard finish or an oil finish.

A hard finish is ultra shiny, like polyurethane wood floors. Oil finishes have a more natural look without the more obvious shine. With an oil-based finish, you can feel the grain of the wood by running your hand over the surface. Hard finishes feel smooth.

Mary's Handy Hints

Still not sure what kind of finish your furniture has? Open the kitchen window and turn on the fan, then boil some linseed oil. Drop just a bit on the surface of the wood. If it sits on top, it's a hard surface. If the linseed oil soaks in, the surface has an oil base. Dry immediately (though the linseed oil will not damage the wood).

Treating Hard Finishes

Your hard finish furniture should stay in good shape with a weekly wiping with a barely damp cloth and drying with a soft, clean cloth. Always dust from left to right and right to left, moving with the grain of the wood. Furniture finish is applied much like paint on a car, which is a left to right motion that follows the grain of the wood. Any movement against the grain will leave scratch marks in the finish.

If you decide to use a product on your furniture, try a wax product such as Guardsman Polish or a product recommended by the manufacturer. Make certain the wax does not contain silicone, petroleum distillates, hydrocarbons, mineral spirits (another term for petroleum distillates), or solvents. This is because the chemicals build up on the finish and will deteriorate it.

You may have read that using too much wax or waxing too often causes a buildup on your furniture. We're here to debunk that myth. Wax itself does not cause a buildup; it's chemicals added to the wax that cause the problems. They soften the finish, which then looks dull and cloudy.

Dirty Words

Stay away from products containing silicone. Nothing sticks to silicone, it is difficult to remove, and it can soften the sealant on some finishes. The only way to know if a product contains silicone is to call the manufacturer and ask for the MSDS (material safety data sheet).

Treating Oil, Satin-Gloss, and Low-Gloss Finishes

Oil, satin-gloss, and low-gloss finishes should be treated with cream waxes or liquid cleaning polishes that do not contain silicones. Always use a soft 100 percent cotton cloth (not a towel), buff thoroughly, and dry immediately. How often depends on where you live. In dry and humid climates, these types of furniture need treating three to four times per year to prevent the wood from warping or drying out. Twice a year is fine in other areas. Increase the frequency if you are seeing signs of drying or warping.

Leather and (Not) Lace

Much like leather pants, leather furniture is slick, expensive, and always in style. Here's how to keep your fashion statement clean and looking good:

◆ Never use saddle soap, strong detergents or soaps, oils, furniture polish, ammonia, abrasive chemicals, alcohol, or other harsh cleaners to clean leather, vinyl, or ultra leather.

◆ Immediately clean any spill with a barely damp cloth and luke-warm water with a bit of mild cleanser such as baby shampoo or Woolite, then dry immediately.

◆ Dust your leather furniture weekly.

Mary's Handy Hints

If you have young children, someone in your home with incontinence problems, or pets who tend to piddle on the couch or chair, buy a plastic tablecloth. Turn the tablecloth upside-down on the couch or chair, then lay a body-size bath towel or colorful throw blanket on top. The towel absorbs the urine while the plastic prevents it from soaking through to the fabric.

◆ Deep clean and condition your leather, vinyl, and ultra leather at least twice a year to prevent drying and cracking.

You can find a good leather cleaner and conditioner—where else?—in western supply stores. Ask for cleaners and conditioners to treat soft leather such as vests and pants; don't use cleaners and conditioners made for hard leather such as boots and saddles. Make certain the cleaner won't darken the material and that it contains no silicone, petroleum distillates, or other harsh solvents.

Cleaning Upholstery

Back in the old days, we had to guess how to clean our upholstered furniture—that's why Grandma always had a plastic cover on her couch. Better to have everything covered with a layer of protective (if ugly) plastic than to have to figure out how to clean these expensive pieces of furniture—and possibly end up with faded, wrinkled, or shrunken sofa cushions.

Nowadays, however, many pieces of furniture carry a cleaning code, which may be printed on fabric samples, on a label under the seat cushion, or on hand tags. Now if only you knew what that cryptic S or X stood for.

Don't drag out Grandma's plastic sofa cover quite yet—we'll share with you the secret of the cleaning codes.

W: Use water-based cleaner. Spot clean this fabric with the foam only of a water-based cleaning agent such as a mild detergent or commercial upholstery shampoo. Use sparingly, and avoid over-wetting.

S: Use solvent cleaner. Spot clean this fabric with a mild water-free dry-cleaning solvent available in local stores. Use sparingly in a well-ventilated room with no sparks or flame in the room.

S-W: Use water-based or solvent cleaner. Spot clean this fabric with a dry-cleaning solvent, mild detergent foam, or upholstery shampoo, depending on the stain.

X: Vacuum only. Clean this fabric only by vacuuming or light brushing to prevent accumulation of dust and grime. Water-based foam or solvent-based cleaning agents of any kind may cause excessive shrinking, fading, or spotting.

Mary's Handy Hints

Whenever you clean upholstery with a detergent, whether you do it yourself or have it done professionally, rinse the cleaned areas with ½ cup of white vinegar per gallon of water. The vinegar removes the soap residue to prevent dirt from clinging to the cleanser left in the fabric. It will stay cleaner far longer.

Now that you broke the code, you can whip off those ugly plastic furniture protectors and actually use your furniture for its intended purpose!

But remember: the use of water-based solvent cleaners may cause spotting or excessive shrinking. Solvent cleaning agents will not remove water stains. Always test an inconspicuous spot first.

Cleaning the Curtains (and Blinds and Shades)

Y'know how in the old movies, the good guy would say to the villain, "It's curtains for you, you fiend!" Well, you're certainly not a fiend, but curtains (and blinds, and shades) are still for you. They keep sunlight from fading your furnishings, let in light when you want it, and even help keep your home warm in the winter and cool in the summer. So it makes sense that you'd want to keep these fantastic creations clean.

Curtains

Vacuum your curtains monthly with the upholstery nozzle, with the vacuum set at the lowest suction. Use short, repeated strokes and move from top to bottom. Clean the nozzle first with sudsy water to remove any dirt that might transfer to the curtain. Allow the bristles to completely dry before vacuuming the curtain.

When vacuuming isn't quite doing it anymore, launder or dry clean your curtains following the instructions on the label. If they're launderable, use the gentlest washer cycle with cool water; draperies can be pretty delicate—constant exposure to light causes the fabric to deteriorate—and they're not likely to be super dirty. Even better, wash the curtains in the tub with Woolite. Dry the draperies on a clothesline.

Mini-blinds

Turn the slats downward facing you. Spray a soft cloth with an all-purpose cleaner. (An old but clean cotton tube sock placed over one hand makes this job whiz by in seconds.) Start at the top and wipe over the surface. Reverse the slats, then pull the blinds out and walk behind them. Repeat from the back. It only takes three or four minutes per blind, so do one room every time you dust to keep ahead of the buildup.

If mini-blinds have (almost) reached the point of no return, grab a hammer and two good-size nails. Measure the blinds and hammer the nails into the back of your home 1 foot less than the width of the blinds. Hang the blinds from the nails and turn the slats downward. With a spray bottle of foaming tub and tile cleaner, begin spraying your way from the bottom to the top. When the cleaner starts dripping from the top, wipe with a wet sponge. Reverse the slats, flip the blinds over, and repeat from the back. Dry and rehang.

This trick only works if you own your own house, condo, or townhouse. Everyone else is stuck with cleaning them in the bathtub and wiping them slat by slat. Lay down enough nonslip pads in the bathtub to cover the floor of the tub. Fill the tub with warm (not hot) water, adding a bit of hair shampoo to the water. Clean the slats one by one with a sponge. Rinse and dry the blinds on a large beach towel, then rehang.

To clean dingy cords, take a handful of white (non-gel) shaving cream and rub it into the cords. Let it sit for ½ hour, then rinse with a solution of ¼ cup vinegar to 1 quart of water.

Wooden Blinds

You can clean wooden blinds using ¼ cup of white vinegar per quart of water instead of all-purpose cleaner. Follow the directions for cleaning mini-blinds with a cloth or sock. Do this regularly—at least once per month—otherwise dirt deteriorates the sealant, causing the blinds to dull.

Fabric Pleated Shades

Fabric pleated shades can't tolerate cleaning chemicals or even water; either will leave unsightly stains. If you vacuum your pleated shades, be sure to wipe the bristles of the brush frequently. The easier way is to wipe the shades down with a chemically treated dry sponge. (See Appendix B for info on where to buy.) Use the sponge dry and wipe over the shades. It's amazing how much dirt it removes!

Vertical Shades

The dry sponge works best for vertical shades. They can be difficult to vacuum because the dirt gets easily embedded into the fabric. You can also roll the shades with a lint roller, although we've found that most vertical shades don't collect dust like horizontal shades.

Problems arise when bugs crawl across the fabric blinds, leaving their, for lack of better terminology, "bug spit" behind. For stains on the shades, dampen a cotton swab with water, then dip it in some liquid dish soap. (The cotton swab helps prevent too much dish soap from getting on the shade.) Wipe it on the stain, let it set for about 30 minutes, then gently blot with a lightweight cloth like an old but clean cotton T-shirt.

Mary's Handy Hints

Use a dry sponge or a brand new ½-inch paintbrush to remove cobwebs and other such nuisances from the top of blinds and shades.

Don't Sweat the Small Stuff

"Don't sweat the small stuff" is a saying, probably invented by hippies or some such that means that you should keep things in perspective and not let small annoyances get you down. In the same way, your living room is filled with "small stuff" such as lampshades, knickknacks, and paintings. Don't let them get you down! We show you how to clean them easily. (And peace, brother!)

Lampshades

Many experts advise cleaning cloth lampshades with the small brush attachment of a vacuum cleaner. "Ha!" we say. Isn't that the same brush you just used to remove dog hair from the La-Z-Boy—and now you want to use it to clean your nice cloth shades? Even if you do wash it prior to using it on the cloth shades, the dirt may still transfer. Also, the bristles on some of these attachments are too coarse to safely use on shades.

Mary's Handy Hints

If you prefer to stick with your brush attachment when cleaning lampshades, here's a simple solution. Cut off the leg of an old pair of panty hose and slide it over the brush rubber, attaching it to the handle with a rubber band. Move the panty hose leg as it soils.

A pastry brush or paintbrush made from horse hair is the safest way to dust cloth, silk, and pleated shades. Follow the dusting with a going-over with a chemically treated dry sponge. These do an excellent job picking up dust and dirt that tends to stick to the shade. Turn the sponge on its edge to work between the folds of the shade.

Use a soft cotton cloth for dusting and cleaning glass, painted metal, or paper shades. Microfiber can scratch metal and plastic shades.

Metal, plastic, and some stitched lampshades can be washed in the tub, but follow the manufacturer's cleaning directions. Metal can rust (remember what happened to the poor Tin Man?), so these shades must be dried quickly. Here are the directions:

1. Lay a rubber nonslip pad in the bottom of the tub.

2. Begin filling the tub with lukewarm water, adding just a bit of Woolite for clothes or baby shampoo. (Liquid dish soap and many detergents are strong cleaners and can damage these shades.)

3. Wash the shade with a soft sponge. (Use only a soft cloth to clean stitched lampshades.)

4. Rinse.

5. Turn the lampshade upside down on a soft cloth so all the water runs out of any seams, taking extra precautions with metal shades so they don't rust in the seams. Heat from a hair dryer helps.

Wash glass shades in the sink, covering the bottom of the sink with a rubber pad to prevent accidental breakage. Clean according to the previous steps.

Glass shades and light fixtures that have gold-plated metal bands can't be washed in the sink. Clean them on the counter on top of a bath towel. Lightly spritz a soft cloth such as a T-shirt with alcohol, then wipe a section at a time, drying immediately to prevent the plating from tarnishing.

Glass Ceiling Fixtures

Glass ceiling fixtures need love, too! A feather duster makes quick work of cobwebs, but that still leaves the glass looking foggy (although not foggy enough for you to drag out a ladder and risk life and limb to clean them). After removing the cobwebs with the feather duster, take a clean cotton tube sock and pull it down over the duster. Spritz one side of the sock with straight rubbing alcohol, which dries quickly and leaves a great shine. Leave the other side dry. Clean the glass with the damp side, then turn it to the dry side to dry.

Ceiling Fans

You can use your handy fan brush, which has an extension pole and bendable head, to give the ceiling fan blades a good dusting. For a more thorough cleaning, don't put away the feather duster and socks quite yet. (Bet you never knew socks were such multitaskers!)

Use a separate sock pulled over the duster to clean your ceiling fans. Lightly spray the sock with a solution of ¼ cup white vinegar per quart of water. Bend the duster to fit over and under the fan blades, then run the duster across each blade. This method does a great job on the base of the fan as well—just use plain water with no vinegar to keep from tarnishing any gold plating on the fan base.

Paintings

For glass-covered pictures, lightly spritz a clean, soft cloth with window cleaner, then wipe over the glass, being careful not to touch the framing. Newer frames can be gently wiped monthly with a dry soft cloth.

Oil paintings? Just leave them alone. Do not use a brush vacuum attachment or blow on them to remove dust. Keep the feather dusters tucked away, as the oil from the duster and the dust previously collected on the duster will damage the painting. If you must, any accumulated dust can be brushed away with an unused artist brush made from horsehair or boar's hair. Any other fiber can scratch the painting.

Cleaning Quips

"God made rainy days so gardeners could get the housework done."

—Author unknown

Even if the beauty of the painting takes your breath away, keep your breath to yourself—the moist air will deteriorate the oil. If you live in an area of high humidity, run a dehumidifier during humid months to keep your painting safe.

Knickknacks

So you decided to ignore our recommendation to keep knickknacks and doodads behind glass. You'll need to dust them two to three times a week with a feather duster to keep the grime away, or clean them individually once a week with a soft cotton cloth. Do not use microfiber because it will eventually scratch away the paint on any painted surface, including figurines.

If your figurines are particularly dirty, you'll need to wash them. Partially fill a plastic tub with warm water, adding a squirt of baby shampoo; dishwashing detergent is too strong for delicate figurines.

Let them soak for a minute, then clean with a 100 percent cotton cloth. Use a cotton swab to reach into the small crevices. We use toothbrushes in many places throughout this book, but we don't use them here—they'll scratch the paint and remove any gold trimming. Also don't clean figurines or crystal knick knacks in the dishwasher; the heat is too intense for these delicate items.

Clean small cloth items by placing them in a laundry bag with a barely damp cloth. Run them for 5 to 10 minutes in the dryer on the air setting—no heat. Don't use a vacuum cleaner brush to clean cloth knickknacks, as the dirt from the brush, even if it has been cleaned, can transfer to the cloth. A clean dry sponge also works quite well to remove dust from cloth figurines.

The Least You Need to Know

- ◆ De-cluttering makes cleaning easier.

- ◆ Thanks to the magic of fabric codes, it's easy to find out how to clean your upholstered furniture.

- ◆ To get your wood furniture clean, you need to know whether it's a hard finish or an oil finish.

- ◆ Don't sweat the small stuff! With the right tools—paint brushes, shampoo, a dry sponge or two—you can keep your lampshades, knickknacks, and other small items clean.

Part 3

The Big Stuff

You probably spend all your cleaning time on dusting knick-knacks and picking up toys, books, and other miscellanea. But the big stuff needs love, too! From the floor to the ceiling, from the windows to the walls, from the attic to the garage, the big things in your home need at least occasional care. Even the air in your home could use freshening up every once in a while! In this part, we tell you how to turn mountains (big stuff such as walls and windows) into molehills (easy cleaning tasks) so that you can finish fast and enjoy a glass of lemonade.

Chapter 8

Floored by Cleanliness

In This Chapter

- ◆ Prescribing rug Rx
- ◆ Pining for clean wood floors
- ◆ Making vinyl vibrant
- ◆ Stone-cold cleaning for stone floors

"Don't tread on me." "She walked all over him." "That dog is always underfoot."

If you don't like being walked on, trod on, or always underfoot, imagine how your floors must feel! You trek through the outdoors, getting all sorts of gunk stuck to your shoes, then you come back inside and mercilessly grind that gunk into the poor floors.

Even worse, when you try to make amends and return the floor to pristine condition, you often use the wrong cleaning solutions and wear away the floors' protective coverings. And if you have pets—well, you know what they can do.

Tell your floor to fear no more. When you reach the end of this chapter, you'll know everything you need to keep your floors happy, whether they're covered in carpet, topped with tiles, or housed with hardwood.

From Haggard Shag to Clean Carpet

When you meander across a grassy lawn, for example, you pick up sand, dirt, and all kinds of squished bugs. When those shoes meet up with the grease and oils in the carpet, the sand, grit, and bug parts become stuck to the grease. No vacuum in the world can suck up that mess!

Even if you work in a hermetically sealed environment that's devoid of dust and dirt, your shoes are still tough on carpet fibers, wearing them down quickly.

Let's say you call a professional carpet cleaner to clean the carpet, and he does a fantastic job, making the carpet look brand new. Two weeks later, though, your carpet is dirtier than it was before he came!

What confounded your cleaning efforts? Unfortunately, the soap used to clean the carpet wasn't completely rinsed out, and this soap created a great nesting ground for dirt. The same thing happens if you don't rinse all the shampoo out of your hair; by the end of the day, you'll have enough grit sticking to the shampoo to build yourself a sand castle.

Mary's Handy Hints

To blot a stain in carpet without causing the carpet fibers to end up with that fuzzy look, dampen a towel in a solution of ½ cup of vinegar to one quart of water. Make a knuckle with the index finger of your right hand and poke it into the towel with your wrist facing to your right. Twist your hand clockwise—the same direction carpet fibers are twisted—then lift your hand and turn it back to the starting position; repeat until the stain is nothing but a memory.

By now, you might be sobbing for the sins you've perpetrated on your carpet. Don't fret! You can use the solutions that follow to become a clean carpet convert and keep your wall-to-wall on the ball.

Are You a Sox Fan?

The first step to keeping clean, as always, is to keep from getting dirty in the first place. If you kick off your shoes before stepping on the carpet, you'll avoid dirtying it with grit, oil, and squished up bug bits.

Oil from the bottom of your feet can also damage carpet after long periods of exposure, so you might consider changing into a clean pair of socks at the same time you step out of the shoes. If not, you could slip on a pair of soft-soled slippers that are worn only inside the house. Your feet will stay warm, and dirt on your shoes will go no farther than the doorstep.

Sucking Up the Dirt

Even if you do ditch the shoes at the door, dirt and dust will travel from your coat and other clothes into the carpet. To keep down the dust, vacuum high-traffic areas of your carpet daily and do a thorough vacuuming of the entire carpet every other week. Every day seems like a lot of work, but we recommend it especially if you have pets or kids, or if you work at home and the carpet gets a lot of traffic from the outside. If that seems like a lot of vacuuming to you, judge how often you need to vacuum the carpet based on how much traffic it gets and how quickly it soils.

Make sure to overlap strokes so you cover the entire carpet, and move heavy furniture away from the walls so you can vacuum behind it.

Change the vacuum bag frequently—even before it's completely full. Why dump it if there's room to spare? Because you often shoot out a cloud of dust when removing a bag that's full to the brim, which defeats the purpose of vacuuming in the first place.

If your family has children or pets, you should sack the bag roughly once a month. (Run the vacuum on a clean floor for a few seconds before you try to change the bag; this will ensure that the vacuum hose is free of dirt that might otherwise get scattered.)

Tape a reminder on the vacuum to change the belt two to three times a year along with the month that it needs changing. Nothing wears down a motor faster than worn belts, which also prevent the beaters from doing the best job they can of picking up dirt. You may need to change the belt more frequently, depending on the number of times you put the machine into action each week.

> **Mary's Handy Hints**
>
> If your vacuum doesn't inhale dirt like it used to, check the bag to see whether it's full. If the bag has room, examine the belt for wear and tear and the beaters for any trapped lint. If those are fine, there might be something caught in the hose; remove the hose from the vacuum, then tape an old cotton tube sock or cloth to the end of a mop handle and run it through the hose. Still not sucking it up? Then it's time to take the vacuum in for a tune-up.

Finishing Rinse

As we mentioned, hiring a carpet cleaning pro can leave you with shampoo-sticky carpets. Instead of turning to the pros for help, you'd be better off renting a steam cleaning machine and doing the work yourself.

Instead of using carpet cleaning shampoo—thereby making your carpet even stickier in the long run—boil some water, then add ½ cup of white vinegar per gallon of water. The hot water in your steam cleaner will reactivate the shampoo that's already stuck in your carpet, and your carpet will end up nice and clean. The vinegar helps dissolve the soap so that it can be pulled up and out of the fibers.

If you've hired a professional shampoo-using carpet cleaner several times, the carpet may feel sticky after the first cleaning with vinegar and water. Don't fret—the shampoo goo will all come out during the second cleaning.

From here on out if you use only vinegar and hot water to clean your carpet, you'll be pleasantly surprised by how clean your carpet stays. Should you decide to hire a professional carpet cleaner, have him rinse the carpet with vinegar and hot water rather than plain water to help lift shampoo out of the rug.

Making Wood Look Good

Homeowners love the look of hardwood floors—the sturdiness, the aged feel that invokes nostalgia for the days of yore—but these floors are hard in name only.

Both hardwood and laminate (i.e., fake wood) floors scratch easily; even sweeping them with a broom can create scratches if the broom picks up a pebble and drags it across the wood. Instead of a broom, reach for a 100 percent cotton mop; the long fluffy strings keep stones and other grit from scraping the floor. If you have large expanses of wood or laminate and the cotton mops seem small by comparison, visit a janitorial supply store and pick up a mightier mop for your home.

Some people recommend using a dusting spray on a cotton dust mop, but over time the spray can build up and make a floor super slick. Worse, the spray can actually damage laminate floors if it's used often.

> **Mary's Handy Hints**
>
> Wood floors will need to be sanded and refinished if they have been damaged by a liquid such as a pet accident that went unnoticed until it soaked in and created a stain. It's also time to break out the sander if the floor has dulled or the boards have warped.

A New Mop Sweeps Clean

There's no right or wrong way to dust or sweep a room. Okay, you could try sweeping with a sharp stick or an ice cream sundae and those efforts are doomed, but we'll assume you have proper tools.

We suggest you start in the corners of a room with a clean paint brush to catch dirt that your mop won't reach. Once you've cleared these areas, move the cotton mop in a figure eight pattern around the edges of the room, then continue to mop out eights in the remainder of the room. Most people prefer to dust in a straight line to make sure they don't miss anything, but as long as you dust every surface, your mop style is a winner.

Using Kid Gloves on New Wood

Dusting is a breeze, but picking up stains off wood floors requires a bit more work, especially with new wood and laminate floors. You want to avoid using excess moisture on these floors as the water works its way down between the boards, eventually causing them to warp after long-term exposure to water.

Instead of slopping out water from a bucket, lightly spritz a terrycloth towel with a mixture of vinegar and water (¼ cup white vinegar per quart of water). Mop the floor with this towel, refolding the towel as needed when the exposed section gets dirty.

This process might sound time-consuming, but if the towel is just lightly dampened, you won't need to dry the wood floors. (If the towel leaves water behind that's still visible after three to four minutes, mop only a small section at a time and use a second towel to dry that section before you move on.)

Newer wood and laminate floors generally don't need waxing. In fact, aside from creating an unattractive film on top of the sealant, waxing a laminate floor might even void your warranty! Not only that, but it will ruin the sealant, and then the floor has to be replaced because laminate floors can't be repaired.

Dirty Words

The vegetable soap used in Murphy's Oil Soap and similar products sticks to hardwood floors, which over time causes the sealant to become gummy. Eventually the entire floor will become so sticky underfoot that it needs refinishing. You can't sand and refinish laminate flooring, so if you use these products long enough on your faux wood, you might need to replace the entire floor!

Counting the Rings While Cleaning

Wood floors that are 35 to 100 years old require different care than their newfangled cousins. You still want to dust them weekly with a cotton dust mop. To clean up small spills, use the vinegar-and-water solution mentioned in the previous section, then dry that part of the floor immediately.

To clean the entire floor, place the vinegar-and-water solution into a spray bottle, and lightly spritz the cotton dust mop to barely dampen it. Damp mop your floor, then launder the dust mop.

Unlike modern wood, older wood floors need to be treated with paste wax two to three times annually to maintain their luster. Make sure that the paste wax is designed for use on hardwood floors! Not all waxes are created equal, and you don't want to be surprised after a lot of hard work. You can wax small areas with a household buffer or by hand with clean cloths, but for large surfaces, you should consider borrowing a large buffing machine from a rental company.

Loving Your Linoleum

It is best to use a nylon broom for dusting. The angle brooms reach into corners easier and shed less than *corn brooms*. They also pick up finer dust than corn brooms with less chance of scratching the floor. Make sure the broom has soft flagged ends.

> **Tidy Terms**
>
> A **corn broom** is a broom made from a plant called broomcorn. When the broomcorn grows it resembles regular corn but there are fibers that form at the end. Those fibers are then tufted to make a corn broom. If they are being used to sweep a floor, especially wood floors, it's best to use ones that are made in the traditional way to prevent scratching the surface. You can find corn brooms at North Woven Broom Co.: www.northwovenbroom.com or 1-866-471-1117.

Use a terrycloth towel and clean these floors with hot water. Add ¼ cup of white vinegar per gallon of water for a cleaning boost if desired. If the floor has deep grooves, borax usually does a good job cleaning. It will not soften and damage the sealant like the phosphorous found in most cleaners. Detergents can't be rinsed off a floor. The sticky residue deteriorates the sealant causing the floor to dull and become difficult to clean. Fill a sink with hot water and half a cup of borax. Scrub the floor with a nylon scrub brush, and then rinse with white vinegar and water.

If your floor has dulled and is not coming clean, then it could be time to strip and wax. I recommend purchasing your floor stripper, sealant, and nonyellowing wax from a janitorial supply store. The supplies are more expensive but replacing your floor costs considerably more. You will be well pleased with how much easier they are to use and the lasting results.

Strip the floor following bottle directions. Then mop with ½ cup vinegar per gallon of water. Apply the sealant, allow it to thoroughly dry, then add two coats of wax waiting for each to dry before applying the next layer. A sealer is necessary or the wax won't give the proper results.

Saving Your Stone Floors

Marble and granite floors require a cotton dust mop to prevent scratches.

Wash stone floors, whether they're tile, marble, granite, or slate, with hot water only—no detergent, no vinegar, no nothing. If you use any kind of detergent on a marble or granite floor, it will deteriorate the shiny surface. On tile, it will seep into the pores. The sticky residue then attracts dirt and the buildup begins. Over time, the detergent softens the adhesive on the back of the tile, causing them to loosen. Vinegar will actually pit these surfaces, and dirt will find its way into the pits.

To clean the floor, mop a small section, then immediately go back and dry it because stone flooring spots easily.

Grout stains are a common problem but can be difficult to remove. Grout is porous, so most cleaners soak right through. Sudsy water and a toothbrush will help. Immediately wipe after any spill. Prevention is always the key to easy cleaning, and this is true for tile grout. Seal your grout after getting it clean. Apply a five-year grout sealer. Wait three to four days and seal it again. Wait another three to four days, then spray a bit of water on the grout. If it stays on top, the grout is sealed. If it soaks through, apply a third coat.

Ceramic Tile Floors

Tile floors can be swept with a broom or vacuumed. Once a week, wash your glazed ceramic tiles with a terry towel and a little detergent. Buff the ceramic tile dry to prevent streaking.

Tiles need a little pepping up? Rub them with half a lemon and buff well. With the other half of the lemon, make lemonade (juice of half a lemon, two tablespoons of sugar, a glass of water, and ice). Enjoy!

The Least You Need to Know

- Shuck the shoes when you enter the house, and your carpets will be much easier to clean.

- Expose wood floors to water as little as possible to keep the wood on the straight and narrow.

- Vinegar (and water) goes well with vinyl and linoleum to keep them looking great; use borax when needed to get into the grooves.

- The only things that should go on a stone or tile floor are your feet and hot water; avoid detergents to avoid long-term damage.

Chapter 9

Walls, Ceilings, and Windows

In This Chapter

◆ Wiping the walls

◆ Hitting the ceiling

◆ Using the pros' secrets for streak-free windows

◆ Tackling tricky ceilings

You clean everything *in* your house, but what about the things that make up your house—the walls, ceilings, windows, and woodwork? They may seem like they never get dirty, but we beg to differ. Look up in a corner where the wall meets the ceiling. See those cobwebs? Case closed.

Then there are the walls themselves, which are easily stained with oils, dirt, and even your young artist's crayons. And as for windows, you may say, why bother? They always end up all streaky anyway.

Well, we say it doesn't have to be that way! With the handy tips in this chapter, you will soon include chores like cleaning walls and windows in your cleaning regimen.

Ceiling Cleaning

The word *ceiling* stems from the Latin root meaning "always overhead, yet always forgotten." Okay, so we made that up. But don't let that meaning come true for you! Clean your ceilings twice a year, or more often if you smoke. Here's the scoop on cleaning flat ceilings, acoustical or "popcorn" ceilings, other textured ceilings, and wood beams.

Flat, Painted Ceilings

Follow these steps to make your ceilings sparkle:

1. Get ready. Remove all wall hangings, curtains, and blinds. Move furniture to one side of the room, then lay down sheets or, preferably, a canvas drop cloth. Use cloth rather than plastic, because plastic can get slippery when wet. Besides, how are you going to move the plastic without dumping dirty water all over the floor?

2. Mix it. Mix 1 cup of borax into a gallon of water, then add ¼ cup of dishwasher detergent.

3. Section it. Do sections of the room at a time. After cleaning the ceiling, wash the surrounding walls.

4. Get cleaning. Clean the ceiling section by section using a clean, soft cloth. Don't use microfiber, which can scratch the paint off the wall.

5. Rinse. Rinse the ceiling as you clean with a second bucket of water plus ½ cup of white vinegar, and dry immediately.

Goodbye, cobwebs … hello clean! Now when you look up, you'll see nothing but a beautiful expanse of ceiling.

Popcorn, Textured, and Wood Beam Ceilings

To clean popcorn ceilings and wood beams, slip three lint roller replacement tubes over the metal base of a paint roller. Attach the roller to your extension handle and roll the ceiling or wood beams to remove dust and cobwebs without smearing the cobwebs or scattering spackling compound everywhere. Duct tape the end of the paint roller to protect the walls from being marred by the roller.

Cleaning the Walls

If dirty walls are, well, driving you up the wall, you came to the right place. Try these tips for removing common snafus from your walls:

- Remove small mars and marks by rubbing gently with an art gum eraser.

- No art gum eraser on hand? Rub the mark gently with toothpaste. Rinse with mouth wash and floss. (Just kidding!)

- Pour a few tablespoons of baking soda into a small container and add enough hydrogen peroxide to make a paste. Apply and let it set for five minutes; this will "bubble" off the stain. Then gently blot with a clean cloth.

- To remove ink, spray a bit of rubbing alcohol on a clean, soft white cloth and blot it on the mark. Wait five minutes and gently blot to remove. Repeat if necessary.

Tackling Tougher Stains

If you're dealing with stains from grease, oil, or crayons, well, that's a tougher cookie to chew.

Try a Mr. Clean cleaning sponge, which does a great job of removing most stains on walls. Rinse with a 50/50 solution of white vinegar to water. Use caution, because the sponge can remove the paint; wipe gently. This sponge also removes crayon and some black magic marker stains.

 Dirty Words

Never use mineral spirits, liquid dish soaps, or WD-40 to remove grease or oil. These products leave a sticky residue, which causes the paint to turn gummy the next time you paint the walls.

If the stain refuses to go, try this:

1. Mix a few tablespoons of cornstarch and enough water to make a thick paste.

2. Plaster the spot and wait until the mixture has dried for several hours. As the cornstarch dries it will absorb the oil.

3. Vacuum off the cornstarch with the brush attachment and then wipe off any residue with a barely damp cotton cloth.

4. Combine one teaspoon of Borax, two teaspoons of dishwasher detergent, and enough hair shampoo to make a thick paste. Plaster the spot, wipe off what you can, then rinse with ¼ cup of white vinegar and a quart of water using a barely damp rag. Also see Appendix A for further suggestions.

If the grease decides to be as stubborn as a Missouri mule, you'll have to apply a primer over the grease and then paint the area using some leftover wall paint.

Mary's Handy Hints

You may need to add just a tiny bit of black paint to darken your left-over wall paint so it will blend better with the color on the wall, depending on how long the paint has been there. Remove a small amount of paint from the can, and place it in a clean plastic tub (an old butter tub, for example). Use a flat toothpick to retrieve just a small amount of black paint. Mix until you have a reasonable match for the paint on the wall.

Washing the Walls

A couple of times per year (more often if you smoke), you'll need to wash down the walls. You'll also want to wash them if you plan to paint them. Here's how:

◆ **Be prepared.** Remove all wall hangings, curtains, and blinds. Move furniture away from the walls. Protect your floors with sheets.

◆ **Pick a product.** We don't like using toxic chemicals to clean anything. Trisodium phosphate (TSP) or trisodium phosphate and
ammonia are often recommended to clean walls, especially just
before painting them. If you don't mind severe headaches and
chemical buildup in your home, they do a great job. (A bit of
sarcasm, there.)

Most paint stores carry an excellent cleaner called Non TSP made
especially for cleaning walls before painting them. It cleans as
well as TSP, but it leaves the toxic chemicals at the manufacturing
plant.

Borax also does an excellent job cleaning walls. Use 1 cup per gallon of water, then add ¼ cup of powdered dishwasher detergent.

◆ **Sponge them.** Always wash
your walls with a natural
sponge carried by paint
stores—never a rag, towel,
or any of the flat mops (cotton or microfiber). These can
leave abrasive marks on the
wall or even completely remove
the paint, especially if the wall
is textured.

 **Mary's Handy Hints**

Cut the toes out of clean
but old cotton tube socks
and place the toeless socks
over your wrists to catch the
dripping water before it runs
up your arms and into your
sleeves. Donate the toes to
someone who always has cold
feet.

◆ **Go in order.** Most experts tell
you to wash from the bottom
up to avoid the dirt streaks that drip down from the top. Baloney!
That means cleaning a wall twice rather than once. Instead, work
from the top down. We have a neat trick that will solve the drippy
problem: when washing walls up high, hold a dust pan covered
with a terrycloth hand towel just under the area you're cleaning to
catch those drips.

Wash the wall from right to left and left to right in the same
direction paint is applied. Cleaning in a circular motion goes
against the grain of the paint, making dirt removal more difficult.

◆ **Make sure to rinse.** Rinse walls as you clean with a second
bucket of water plus ½ cup of white vinegar, and dry immediately.
Vinegar not only is an excellent cleaner, but it also has the ability
to remove any cleaner from the wall so paint glides on easily.

No matter what product you use to clean the walls, you should open all the windows and doors in your home and turn on a fan in each room to circulate the fumes out of your home. Spring and fall are the best time to do any heavy-duty cleaning like this because you can open the windows and let the fresh air in.

Treating Paneling

Wood paneling, which was popular in rec rooms in the '70s, is making a comeback. Here's how to keep it clean.

All wood paneling, whether it's synthetic, finished, or raw wood, must be dusted regularly. Use either the brush attachment on your vacuum cleaner, a wool duster, or a chemically treated dry sponge.

Then follow the instructions for your type of wood paneling:

+ **Unfinished wood paneling.** Lightly wipe clean using a barely damp cloth. Using moisture on unfinished wood paneling can damage the wood, so wipe with just enough moisture to clean the wood. Wait 24 hours, then apply a wood treatment recommended by the manufacturer.

Dirty Words _____

Never use an oil-based soap to clean wood paneling. The soap leaves a residue on the surface that can soften the finish. You can't apply the necessary wood oil to unfinished wood paneling after using oil soap, as the wood oil won't adhere to a surface cleaned with oil soap.

+ **Sealed or finished wood paneling.** Generally, damp cleaning finished paneling isn't necessary. Using a chemically treated dry sponge should sufficiently remove most surface dirt.

If grime has developed on the paneling, clean using ½ cup of white vinegar per gallon of water or a cleaner recommended by the manufacturer.

Work from the bottom up, cleaning with the grain of the wood. Rinse the sponge as it gets dirty in a separate bucket of clean water. Clean a small section at a time, drying with a clean 100 percent cotton terry towel as you finish that section.

Why bottom up here but top down for painted walls? On sealed or finished wood, any dirty water dripping down onto dirty wood paneling could cause streaking in the finish that is very difficult to remove. If the wall is already clean, it will wipe clean easily without leaving the streaks.

Fireplace Fronts

While you're cleaning the walls, you may as well take care of your brick or stone fireplace front!

1. Saturate the bricks or stones with an all-purpose cleaner and allow it to soak in for a few minutes.

2. Thoroughly spray the bricks or stones with a foaming tub cleaner.

3. Scrub with a stiff bristle brush dipped in a mixture of one squirt of dishwashing liquid and one cup of borax per bucket of water. Reapply the tub cleaner as needed.

4. If the soot refuses to budge, resort to Non TSP cleaner found in paint stores.

Keep the room well ventilated, wear gloves and a mask, and protect your skin, carpet, and any furniture close by. Always cover the area in front of the fireplace with several old sheets and place plastic down on the bricks in the floor.

Cleaning Log Home Walls

When you built houses with Lincoln Logs as a kid, we bet you never thought about how you'd clean those walls! Now you're all grown up with a real log home, and it's time to get those walls clean. How do you do it?

For a light cleaning, dust cobwebs using a lambswool duster; they're bendable to conform to the shape of the log.

When a more aggressive cleaning becomes necessary, use a clean but old cotton tube sock dampened with ½ cup of white vinegar per gallon of water. Place a plastic bag over the lambswool duster and then put the sock over that, fastening it to the handle with a rubber band. Rub the duster over the walls, turning it as it becomes soiled.

When it comes time to deep clean the logs, mix 2 cups of hydrogen peroxide and ½ cup of white vinegar per gallon of water. Grab a partner and begin washing from the top with a sponge. Your partner needs to rinse the walls with plain water and dry immediately. Remember to put drop cloths on the floor and move furniture to the center of the room.

Window Wizardry

Can you see outside the windows of your home? We'll assume the answer is yes. More importantly, can you see the windows themselves? We'll take a chance and assume this answer is also yes.

Whereas other parts of your home show dirt well—thus inspiring a bit of attention from you—dirty windows often seem clean because the sun keeps shining through them. When you take a closer look and see what's on the glass, though, you'll likely be inspired to wipe them clean and let the sun shine even brighter.

And although your grandmother might have had good advice about life in general, don't adopt her window-cleaning style of crumpled newspaper and lots of elbow grease. Instead, follow these pro tips to leave your glass squeaky clean.

From the Inside Out

Cleaning the inside of windows is much easier than the outside, so let's tackle that first. Start by mixing up a batch of our home brew window cleaner, which costs almost nothing to make and leaves no streaks.

 Dirty Words

Never use paper towels or old newspapers to clean a window. Paper contains small amounts of pulp that can scratch glass. Use towels that have been rinsed in white vinegar—not fabric softener—during the rinse cycle because vinegar removes any soap residue that might leave smears on the glass.

In a brand new spray bottle, add ⅓ cup of distilled white vinegar and ¼ cup of rubbing alcohol, then fill the rest of the bottle with distilled water. (Distilled water produces the best results because water content varies greatly from town to town.)

Remove any knickknacks from the windowsill, and push aside the curtains. Spray the cleaner on the windows, then wipe them dry using a soft, 100 percent cotton cloth. Dab the windowsill with another cloth if any liquid lands there, then everything to its original place. No more children's fingerprints and slobbery dog nose prints!

From the Outside In

Whereas the inside cleaning will go quickly, the outside of your windows will take a lot longer. They get rained on and have dirt blown against them, so they're sure to be much dirtier on the outside than the inside.

First you need to be able to get to the windows, so remove the screens and place them on top of a sheet of plastic. Arrange them in the order you take them off so that you'll have no trouble knowing which screen goes where. (You might not want to clean more than one side of the house at a time or else you'll have dozens of screens all over the place.)

Spray the screens with a foaming tub and tile cleaner, then lay them at an angle against the house. When the foam starts to drip down the screens, use a wet sponge to gently wipe them clean. Allow the screens to dry while you tackle the windows.

Mary's Handy Hints

No matter which type of glass cleaner you use, cleaning your windows in the morning or early evening will give you the best results. When glass becomes hot from the sun's rays, the window cleaner will dry too quickly and leave streaks.

When all the screens are in the drip-dry cycle, brush the window sills and framing with a medium-size paintbrush to remove bits of leaves and other debris. Clean the sills and framing with an orange-based cleaner.

To clean the windows themselves, you'll want to take a page from the professionals and use a squeegee, a chamois, and some quick wrist action. Here are the steps:

1. Mix 1 tablespoon of powdered dishwashing detergent, ½ cup of white vinegar, and ⅓ cup of rubbing alcohol in a bucketful of water.

2. Using the cloth head of a squeegee or a separate cloth rag, swab the solution on the window from top to bottom.

3. Use the rubber blade of the squeegee to wipe off the solution. Start by using one corner of the blade to wipe where the top edge of the window meets the frame.

4. Continue to wipe the window in horizontal strokes from top to bottom, with the top of the squeegee slightly ahead of the bottom so that it pushes water down as you move across the glass. Overlap the strokes by an inch so you leave no water behind. At the end of each stroke, wipe the squeegee dry with a lint-free cloth.

5. Remove any water remaining on the sides of the glass with a barely damp chamois, which soaks up water without leaving streaks.

6. Dry the window frame and sill with a rag—not the lint-free cloth or chamois, mind you, but a separate rag meant solely for this purpose. This prevents you from spreading dirt and water back onto the squeegee, and therefore onto the window.

If you've never handled a squeegee before, you will undoubtedly leave streaks of water behind the first dozen or so times you try it. That's okay—it takes only seconds to wipe on more solution and clean the window again. (Cleaning the windows takes just minutes; it's moving the ladder around and sliding storm windows up and down that takes so long.)

After you've finished washing the windows, park yourself in a chair in front of a picture window and enjoy the view!

The Least You Need to Know

◆ Be sure to prepare for washing walls and windows, protect the floors and furniture, and have all your cleaning products on hand.

◆ Remove marks from walls with an art gum eraser, toothpaste, or baking soda mixed with hydrogen peroxide.

◆ Clean popcorn ceilings and wood beams with a few lint-remover replacement tubes on a paint roller.

◆ When washing outside windows, forget the crumpled newspaper and do it like a pro—with a squeegee.

Chapter 10

The Great Outdoors

In This Chapter

- ◆ De-gunking gutters
- ◆ Cleaning the siding
- ◆ Manning the deck (and the patio)
- ◆ Keeping up with the pool duties

Remember how when you were in school your teachers stressed the importance of being well-rounded? This meant that even if you were a jock at heart, you didn't spend all your time on the gridiron or the softball field. And if you were a brain, you had to unbury your nose from your books every so often and get some fresh air.

Well, your home needs to be well-rounded, too. We've spent a lot of time in this book talking about cleaning the inside of your home. But it makes no sense to have a sparkling interior and an exterior that's laden with dirt and mold. That's why in this chapter, we tell you how to clean the *outside* of your home.

Great Gutters

Sometimes it seems like gutters exist merely to trap leaves and other junk so that you have to schlep up there and haul it all out—but really, gutters direct the water from rainfall away from your siding, doors, windows, and foundation. In other words, they keep your home dry!

You need to clean (and repair, if necessary) gutters twice per year. Here's what you'll need to get started:

- Rubber work gloves
- Scrub brush
- Safety glasses
- Ladder
- Gutter seal
- Narrow garden trowel
- Water hose with a high-pressure nozzle
- Plumber's snake
- Chalk
- Caulking gun

Safety First!

Clean gutters aren't worth risking your health over. Always make sure your ladder is firmly anchored. If you'll be on anything taller than a stepladder, have a friend there to steady you; never climb a ladder if no one is at home to help you should you fall off!

Dirty Words

Never lean your ladder against the gutter; this can damage the gutter. Gutter attachments from the hardware store will let you raise the ladder higher than the gutter without damaging it.

Wear heavy work gloves to protect your hands. Many gutters have screws and other pointy bits sticking out into the trough, and you don't want to mess with them while you're cleaning out debris!

Getting Started

Now that we've scared the bejeebers out of you, it's time to get started actually cleaning the gutters. Here's how:

1. Scoop out the gunk. Starting at a drain outlet at the low end of a gutter, scoop out loose debris with the narrow garden trowel, working away from the drain outlet. You can hang a bucket off of a hook on the ladder to dump leaves and other debris into.

2. Hose out the gutters. Using a hose, wash out each length of gutter, working toward the drain outlet. This can be a messy job! If the dirt is stubborn, use a stiff scrub brush to persuade it to come loose.

3. Clear the drainpipes. If your drainpipes don't drain freely, try flushing the blockage down them with the hose. If that doesn't work, climb down your ladder and use a plumber's snake to pull out debris from the bottom.

4. Repair leaks. If water is leaking through seams between gutter sections, mark the leaks with chalk, allow the gutter to dry, then seal the leaks from the inside with gutter seal. After giving the sealant time to dry, spray water down the gutters to make sure the seals are watertight and that the water flows out properly.

5. Check the spikes. Look under the gutter. If you can see daylight between the gutter and the fascia board (the board the gutter is nailed to), the gutter has separated from the house. Pull out the spikes that have loosened and replace them with gutter bolts from the hardware store.

6. Clean the outside. Don't ignore the outsides of the gutters—they'll get jealous! Mix ⅓ cup of powdered laundry detergent and ½ cup of borax in a gallon of water. Add 2 cups of hydrogen peroxide if mold or mildew have begun to attack the outside of the gutters. Wear gloves to protect your hands, and use a white scrub pad to wipe down the gutters. (Don't use any color other than white because they're more abrasive and will scratch the gutter.) A sponge covered with nylon netting works, too.

Taking Sides: Cleaning Your Home's Siding

The outside of your home is exposed to the elements (who knew?), and as such is a target for dirt, mold, and other unsavory characters.

Aluminum Siding

Aluminum siding is metal that's been given a factory paint job. If it's not taken care of, it can oxidize (turn chalky). To head off problems, clean the siding twice a year. Rent or buy a power washer and wash the siding with a specialized siding cleaner from your local home center, or use a solution of laundry detergent and water.

Vinyl Siding

The good news: vinyl siding doesn't split, buckle, or warp. It never needs to be painted (in fact, you *can't* paint it!).

The bad news: vinyl siding etches over the years, causing a dull look and making it prone to stain. You can put the kibosh on vinyl problems by cleaning it twice a year. Rent or buy a power washer, and wash the siding with a specialized siding cleaner (available at home centers) or a solution of laundry detergent and water.

Stucco

Your stucco may turn dark with dirt—or white with *efflorescence*. (This also happens on brick.) Clean your exterior stucco once per year, or more often if it's a light color. Here's the solution, which you can use in a power washer:

Tidy Terms

Efflorescence occurs when the mineral salts in the mortar of your stucco dissolve. It leaves a white appearance that stands out from the rest of the stucco.

2 gallons hot water
2 tablespoons dishwashing soap
½ cup borax
½ cup washing soda

With the hose attachment on the power washer, work the dirt from the top all the way down; if you stop, the leftover grunge will stain the stucco.

Brick

Your brick exterior will stay beautiful with an occasional hosing down. But if you spot moss, mold, or mildew, thoroughly wet the brick with water, then scrub with a solution of 1 cup of 20 percent hydrogen peroxide to 1 gallon of water.

Mary's Handy Hints

Scrub brick with a natural or synthetic bristle brush—never wire. A wire brush can leave behind traces of steel, which can rust and discolor the brick.

Wood

Wood siding looks great, but much like a supermodel, it is high maintenance; it needs painting every five years or staining every three years to protect it. Keep it beautiful longer by cleaning it twice per year.

You can clean wood siding with a power washer, but take caution—the powerful stream of water can remove the paint, so you may need to repaint afterwards.

You can also hand clean the wood with a long-handled soft-bristled brush and a solution of a few squirts of liquid dish detergent in a bucket of water.

All Hands on Deck

You love sitting out on your deck sipping a sweet drink and reading a good book. Don't we all! But it's hard to enjoy yourself when dirt and grime on the deck compete for your attention.

Give deck dirt the brush-off with these tips:

◆ Organic matter such as leaves, helicopter seeds, and twigs can stain your deck. Be sure to sweep such debris off the deck frequently.

◆ If you can't see it, it won't hurt your deck, right? Wrong. Debris that builds up between the boards traps moisture, encouraging scourges such as mildew and rot. Blast out the junk with a high-pressure stream from your hose.

♦ Gas grills are awesome for serving up burgers, chicken, and brats—but they're not so awesome when it comes to leaving permanent grease stains on your deck. Place a nonflammable mat under the grill, and be sure to clean the overflow compartment frequently.

These general tips will help keep your deck brighter longer. Now on to the wood-specific advice.

Cleaning Redwood or Cedar Decks

If your deck is made of redwood or cedar and you don't mind the grayish hue it can take on, simply rinse the deck and scrub it with a stiff-bristle brush to remove grime. If the gray makes you see red, try a deck brightener product, which you can get at many home centers. Spray or brush the brightener on, let it sit for as long as the manufacturer recommends, and rinse.

Dirty Words _____

Be careful around house trim and siding with a power washer—this powerful machine can blow parts of your house away!

Cleaning Pressure-Treated Pine Decks

For woods that don't weather naturally, try a solution of ½ cup of borax and ⅓ cup of powdered laundry detergent per gallon of water. If the dirt is really out of control, rent or buy a power washer to blast it away.

Patios

You want to keep your patio clean—but not at the risk of turning your beautiful surrounding shrubs and flowers into yard waste. We have the environmentally friendly solution. For a concrete patio, first hose down your patio, then apply a mixture of 1 gallon of warm water, 1 cup of white vinegar, and 2 tablespoons of borax with a long-handled brush. Scrub and rinse with the hose. Tile and stone patios can be scrubbed with a mild nonphosphorous cleaner and a scrub brush. And if you have problems with termites, try cleaning your patio with a leaf blower instead of water.

Patio Furniture

Ahh, the great outdoors. It's filled with fresh air, beautiful trees, cute little animals ... and dirt. That's why you need to clean your outdoor furniture every season.

Plastic Furniture

You have a choice when it comes to plastic patio furniture: Learn to live with the stains, or paint it with a special paint made for plastic furniture. Stains in patio furniture will not come out no matter what product you use or the amount of scrubbing your poor elbows endure.

To paint the furniture, wipe off all dust and dirt with a towel. Thoroughly clean it using a bucket of warm water plus ½ cup of borax and ½ cup of laundry soap. Scrub and air dry. Follow the directions on the can of paint, working outdoors with plastic laid down to protect your work surface.

Wicker Furniture

Use a 100 percent lambswool duster or the soft-bristle brushes of a vacuum cleaner to remove dust and cobwebs on wicker furniture.

Clean your wicker furniture four times per year with a bit of liquid dish soap in a bucket of water. Dip a soft cloth—not a terry towel—in the bucket, then wring out most of the moisture. Cleaning wicker with soap and water prevents it from drying and cracking.

 **Mary's Handy Hints**

Cut off 1 to 2 inches of a 2-inch-wide paintbrush to reach into the smaller crevices that the vacuum cleaner won't reach. Removing the top 1 to 2 inches of the paintbrush leaves stiffer bristles that work into the wicker more easily than soft bristles.

Wrought-Iron Furniture

To remove dust and dirt, first use the soft-bristle brush of your vacuum cleaner, then switch to a paint brush as suggested for dusting wicker furniture.

Sure, you can clean wrought iron with water—but if you don't get all the water out from between those intricate details (no easy task), it will rust. However, ionized water is safe because it protects metal from rusting. (Ionized water runs about $9 for a quart bottle, and you need only about ½ cup to do patio furniture.) Take the piece outside and lightly spray the wrought iron with ionized water. Immediately dry with a soft cloth and set the furniture in the sun to finish drying.

Mary's Handy Hints

A protective coat of liquid beeswax mixed with boiled linseed oil on your wrought iron retards rusting and simplifies cleaning jobs.

Banish rust stains by rubbing the wrought iron with kerosene. Let that set 10 to 15 minutes, then scour with a 0000 steel-wool pad. For your health's sake, always use kerosene outdoors. You can also use commercial rust removers.

Aluminum Framing Furniture

Metal polish such as Met-All or Flitz cleans and polishes nonpainted aluminum framing. Use either twice a year for best results. Both polishes do a great job cleaning and polishing nonsealed vehicle wheels, too. You can also clean aluminum framing with a 50/50 solution of white vinegar to water and a good nylon scrub brush.

Painted metal patio framing is best cleaned by mixing ½ cup of borax in a bucket of warm water and scrubbing with a soft nylon scrub brush. If you're really energetic, a toothbrush cleans the small crevices quite nicely.

Fabric Cushions

Clean fabric cushions and pads with a foaming tub and tile cleaner. Spray on the surface and be patient for the next 10 to 15 minutes while the cleaner foams away the grime. Rinse with ½ cup of white vinegar per gallon of water. Air dry.

To remove tree sap from your cushions, first freeze it with an ice cube. Chip off what you can with the blunt side of a kitchen knife. Then try dabbing on a bit of peanut butter to remove the rest, and clean the peanut butter with sudsy water. Do test an area first, as the peanut butter can sometimes stain.

Vinyl Cushions

Clean vinyl patio cushions with a good-quality leather and vinyl cleaner and conditioner. The conditioner will prevent drying and cracking if used twice a year, especially if the vinyl bakes in the sun all summer.

Patio Umbrellas

Open the umbrella and brush off all the dust and dirt, then remove any sap with ice and peanut butter as we described for fabric cushions. Grab that can of foaming tub and tile cleaner, and start spraying from the bottom rim of the umbrella to the center hole until the entire surface is covered with those wonderful scrubbing bubbles. Using a white scrub pad, wipe the entire area, then rinse with a solution of ½ cup of white vinegar to 1 gallon of water. Let the umbrella dry in the sun.

Prepping the Pool

You have a pool? Can we come over?

In all seriousness, a pool presents a major cleaning task. You need to vacuum out leaves, dead bugs, and other debris; clean the filters; scrub the sides; and add all sorts of chemicals that keep the water clean. The following is a quick guide to maintaining your pool; for more information, refer to the manufacturer's cleaning instructions.

> **Mary's Handy Hints**
>
> Keeping your pool's surroundings clean will keep leaves, grass clippings, and so on from blowing into the water or being carried there on the feet of swimmers. Hose down the deck regularly, and rake the surrounding lawn.

Here is a list of *daily* care instructions:

- Test the pool water following the manufacturer's instructions.
- Test the sanitizer level, pH level, and alkalinity.
- Add chlorine or bromine.
- Adjust pH and alkalinity levels.
- Clear debris from the skimmer basket.

The skimmer basket traps large debris before it can get to the filter. Clean it out to keep the pool water circulating freely.

Here is a list of *weekly* care instructions:

- Add algaecide.
- Add a product that sequesters metal particles.
- Add clarifier.

Here is a list of *as-needed* care instructions:

- Shock the pool water. Also known as superchlorinating, shocking is oxidizing everything in the pool. When you raise chlorine levels to 10 times the level of chloramines, the breakpoint chlorination threshold is reached. Everything (such as algae and other impurities) in the pool is oxidized in a "shock." You can shock the water by telling it dirty jokes, but more effective would be to follow the manufacturer's instructions.

- Vacuum the pool. Most manual pool vacuums attach to the skimmer and use pump pressure to bring debris off the bottom of the pool through the filter system.

- Skim off leaves. Use a leaf skimmer attached to the vacuum pole to remove leaves as well as bugs and other flotsam (or is it jetsam?).

- Brush the walls. Use a wall brush to scrub pool walls and bottom. This frees up dirt and debris so they can get caught in the pool's filtration system.

◆ Check the filter/backwash. The filter system removes debris by
trapping small particles that don't dissolve in the pool water. Most
swimming pool filters use sand, diatomaceous earth, or cartridge
elements. Follow the manufacturer's instructions for cleaning or
backwashing.

Now that your pool is sparkling clean, go make a splash!

The Least You Need to Know

◆ You can find products at home improvement stores for cleaning
most kinds of home siding—or you can make your own.

◆ Always take safety precautions when working on a ladder.

◆ Clean your deck, patio, and patio furniture once per year to keep
them sparkling.

◆ You may think you need a chemistry degree to keep a pool clean,
but everything you need to know should be in the manufacturer's
instructions.

Chapter 11

Garages, Attics, and Basements

In This Chapter

- ◆ Cleaning out the garage
- ◆ Attacking the attic
- ◆ Taking the "base" out of basement
- ◆ Turning trash into treasure

If you're working through this book in order, then you've already cleaned up the living room, the kitchen, all your bedrooms, and much more. These are the rooms you live in and walk through every single day, so it's easy to spend a lot making them look perfect.

What remains, though, is a bit more of a challenge: there's the garage, loaded with half-empty bags of fertilizer and old flower pots that you used for a single summer back in 1998; there's the attic, piled high with mementos from your children's school days, a decade's worth of financial records, and old clothes that you're sure you'll wear again some day; and finally there's the basement, a resting ground for old toys, books, and woodworking projects—not to mention everything you removed from the rooms upstairs while you were cleaning them!

You already pushed the dirt and clutter to the edges of your house—now it's time to finish the job! This chapter will help leave your house spotless from the eaves to the foundation.

Clearing Out the Garage

Whenever garages are used for storage, there's always a pattern to how the items accumulate. First, storage hooks and shelves are installed on the back and side walls because those spaces are normally left unused. Why waste the space, right?

You add in hooks to hang ladders and bicycles, then start lining up items in the space between the two cars (assuming you have a two-car garage, that is). The garbage cans, the recycling bins, bags of mulch, peat moss, and topsoil pile up, pushing out into the garage itself. Finally, you leave one of the cars in the driveway—just for today, you tell yourself—to make room for a new riding lawnmower, and before you know it, you're the owner of a no-car garage and the squirrels are setting up house in the corner.

Have no fear—in a single afternoon, you can send the rodents back to nature and reclaim your parking space, while simultaneously spiffing up your garage.

Four Piles, No Waiting

First and foremost, cleaning the garage requires you to clear it of endless piles of cobwebby rubble. For this task, you should avail yourself of the Four Pile Method. As you might deduce from the name, you'll divide your belongings into four piles, and each pile will meet a different fate.

Ideally, as you separate your belongings, you should pile them outside the garage so that you can clean the actual building before things go back into it. We'll get to the cleaning after the piles, and the categories are as follows:

- **Good, verging on great.** This pile is for things you use often that need to be accessible, such as lawn tools, sprinklers, garbage cans, and bicycles. You use these items on a regular basis, so they should stay within arm's reach (ergo, within the garage).

- **Good—but not right now.** Does your snow shovel collect dust for eight months and get underfoot whenever you reach for a rake? Are the inner tubes you save for that annual trip down the river getting grimy? Instead of letting this stuff hog space that could be used on a daily basis, pack it in boxes or wrap it in large plastic bags and store it in the attic, basement, or shed. You'll reclaim space and keep the items clean until you need them again.

  Cleaning Quips

  "A broad margin of leisure is as beautiful in a man's life as in a book. Haste makes waste, no less in life than in housekeeping. Keep the time, observe the hours of the universe, not of the cars."
  —Henry David Thoreau

- **Good—but not that good.** If you don't use something anymore—old flowerpots, a portable grill, a stand-up net that acts as a base-ball catcher—yet it's still in good shape, pass it on to a friend or donate it to the Salvation Army. (Call your local branch to find out whether they do pick-ups or whether you need to drop off the goods.) If you can't bear the thought of giving away your precious left ski (the one that reminds you how you broke the right one) or broken beta-max VCR, hold a garage sale and rake in a few bucks while you clean house.

  Mary's Handy Hints

  If you do decide to hold a sale to clear out your garage, contact your town hall to see whether you need a permit. When you do this, ask where and how long you can hang signs to promote the sale.

- **Goo ... uh, never mind.** All too often, we set something aside with a promise to restore it to perfection later: the old gas-powered lawnmower that sputters and dies, or a table that we bought at a garage sale that needs just a tiny little bit of sanding, touching-up, staining, and varnishing.

Enough's enough—give yourself until the end of the day to restore these items to their former glory. If they're still darkening your driveway come sunrise, get rid of them! Put them out with the trash, or if they're large items, call your local sanitation department to make arrangements for pick-up. You can even haul items to the curb and place a large "Free" sign on them. If someone else wants to adopt your albatross, help him load the items in his truck and wish him well!

Oil's Well That Ends Well

Cars use oil, and although we tend to view oil as a precious commodity, they have a pesky habit of leaking that oil onto our clean garage floors.

Now that you've cleared everything out of the garage, you might have a fresh view of a stain long forgotten. To get rid of it, you can scrub in a concrete stain remover such as Zep. If the Zep doesn't zap it, grind kitty litter into the stain with a brick or your foot. Let the powder stand for several hours, then sweep it up. The kitty litter will absorb the stain like magic! We tried this trick with an unidentified stain on concrete that even the Zep couldn't get out, and it worked great.

You Can Rebuild It

After you've reduced four piles down to one, it's time to move everything back into the garage … almost. Before you grab things and start flinging, you need to clean the space first. Then you can establish some kind of order so that the garage never returns to chaos. Here's what we suggest:

- ◆ **Sweep it clean.** While your garage is still empty, grab a broom and sweep the walls and rafters to put the kibosh on spider webs. Start from the top and work your way down, using a push broom for the floor to leave every surface sparkling clean—well, as sparkling as a garage can be.

- ◆ **Go vertical.** Use the walls as storage space so that your precious and limited floor space remains free. Hang bikes and ladders on hooks, install shelves for gardening tools, and hang tools on pegboard. Wrap skis and lay them across the rafters instead of standing them in the corner.

♦ **Group like items.** Group like items (gardening gloves, plant food, trowels, etc.) together so that everything you need for a certain activity is all in one place.

♦ **Recycle.** If your town offers recycling services, place the recycling bins in the garage near the door to the house (if you have an attached garage) to make it easier to toss in bottles, cans, and paper.

♦ **Can the small stuff.** To keep track of little items such as nails, screws, and garbage bag twist-ties, nail the lids of peanut butter or other plastic jars onto a rafter or another horizontal surface. Fill the jars themselves with the screws, nails, or whatever, and screw them onto the lids. Voilà! Instant storage that's out of the way, yet still easy to reach.

Disposing of Toxic Messes

Does your garage still have a can of lighter fluid that the previous owner left behind? Are you storing old oil from the past four changes because you're not sure what to do with it?

These and other products in your garage might be considered hazardous waste, so check with your local hazardous waste facility or recycling center to find out how to dispose of these items. You might have to pay a fee to get these items out of your hair (so to speak), but the few dollars you'll pay is a small price compared to the environmental damage these wastes could cause if they enter the water system.

Cleaning the Attic

You've heard of people who discovered Grandma's old settee in the attic, brought it to an antique shop or the traveling TV program *Antiques Roadshow*, and found out it's a 1706 Snobworthy Settee worth $15,000. Well, this can happen to you—if you clean out your attic and find out what's hiding among the insulation.

Here are the steps to take to turn your upper story into a place of glory:

1. **Lift and shift.** Move everything to one side of the attic. Although attics aren't usually a comfortable place to spend time, you don't want to have to lug furniture and other heavy items down and back up the attic stairs. By shifting everything to one side, you give yourself a place to sort your stash.

Dirty Words _____

Get someone to help you move heavy items. Attics typically have low ceilings, so you'll be crunched in an unusual position just to walk around. Don't risk pulling a muscle as well by trying to move a trunk or heavy box on your own!

2. **Bring on the piles.** As you move things, sort them into piles: items to keep, items to give away, and items to toss. (Your attic is already a storage space, so the Four Pile Method creates one too many piles here.) Be ruthless! If you haven't used an item in years, chances are you won't need it anytime in the near future.

3. **Clean up.** After you've cleared a space, use a dust mop and a broom with a cleaning cloth over the bristles to clean the floor, ceiling, rafters, and walls. Use the tips in Chapter 8 for cleaning wood floors. (Consider wearing a face mask if your attic has exposed insulation. No need to breathe any of the particles and fibers you might kick up while sweeping.)

   If you have a brick chimney, check the mortar in between the bricks to see if it's crumbling; if so, arrange for someone to replace the mortar before the next cold season.

4. **Spot the animals.** Look for signs of pests, such as mouse pellets or dead insects, while you move boxes. If you find anything, either set out traps or call a pest control professional.

5. **Finish the job.** Restack everything that you're keeping. Label every box so that you won't have to open it in the future to know what's inside; add as much description as you can. Set heavy boxes against the walls, then place smaller and lighter boxes on top of them for easy access (and less crushing action).

Place everything you're giving away or tossing into plastic bags, and bring the bags downstairs, preferably moving them out the door immediately, whether to a charity organization or an antique shop. After all, as soon as you set something down, there's a chance you might just leave it there!

Banishing Basement Dirt

It's dark, it's dusty, it's cobwebby—but your basement doesn't *have* to resemble a stage set from a Vincent Price horror flick. Follow these tips to turn your grungy old basement into a bright and clean storage area:

1. **Prep yourself.** If you suffer from allergies and have an unfinished basement, you'll want to have dust masks on hand. You may also want to cover your head with a cloth to keep the dust from raining down on you from above. Finally, have all your cleaning tools ready at the bottom of the basement stairs.

2. **Let there be light.** If your basement is dim, turn on all the lights, then dust and clean any windows to let in as much light as possible. Bring in floor lamps from upstairs if you need to. You can't tackle dirt if you can't see it!

3. **Pull together the piles.** Starting in the area the farthest away from the stairs, make a sweep of the basement, repeating the three-pile process that you did in the attic. (You should be a massing master by this time, able to pile a pile like nobody's business.)

   Move whatever you're tossing or donating out of the area, then shift everything else into another room or part of the basement. Label boxes so you'll know what's what; if you don't have everything in boxes, visit a liquor store or supermarket for all the free boxes you can handle, and pack up everything. Cleaning a flat box top is much easier than cleaning just about any other surface.

4. **Sweep it down.** Making sure your head cloth and dust mask are in place, use a broom to sweep cobwebs down from the ceiling and rafters—watch out for spiders! Work through one area at a time. When all the dirt is on the floor in one area, sweep it up into a dustpan and toss it. Mop the floor afterward with a good cleaning product.

As in the attic, look for evidence of pests (mouse droppings, tiny bits of wood resulting from termite damage, chewed-up boxes) and turn to traps or an exterminator if you find anything.

5. **Stop the spores.** A musty odor means mold—and when mold has a hold on your basement, you'll need to take radical action to keep it from spreading. After all, mold can wreak all kinds of havoc on your health, including adult-onset asthma, bronchitis, sinusitis, and headaches.

   Treat moldy and mildewy areas with straight 20 percent hydrogen peroxide. If a box of books smells like mildew, isolate it from other boxes or send it straight to the recycling plant. If mold has taken control of the entire area, you may have to move everything out of the basement to seal the floors or walls.

   If your basement is humid, purchase a dehumidifier to remove water from the air, which will in turn help prevent mold and mildew from forming. You might also consider using heavy-duty plastic storage containers to keep items from getting musty.

6. **Pitch the paint.** As in the garage, you might discover plenty of leftover chemicals, cleaners, and other toxic items while cleaning the basement. Again, call the hazardous waste department to find out how to dispose of these items properly.

   One item of special note for basements is paint. If you like to change the color of your rooms often, your basement will look like a Sherwin Williams franchise in no time if you don't know how to dispose of leftover paint.

   Some recycling centers have sections in their "swap shops" for oil-based paint, because this paint stays good for long periods of time. You might be able to drop off old cans and find out if your neighbors share your taste in colors.

   As for latex paints, these separate after a short while, turning them into sticky, gooey trash—but you can't just throw them in a trash bag or else paint will explode all over the place once the garbage truck tries to compact the cans. Thankfully, you can buy a hardening agent that will turn the goopy stuff into a solid mass, which you can then dispose of safely. (Clumping cat litter often does the trick as well, so weigh the prices of each product depending on how many cans you need to nix.)

7. **Close off the cellar.** As you clean and mop sections of the basement, move items back in, stacking light items on top of heavy with the labels facing out.

If you use your basement as a workshop or place to do other hobbies, think about what kinds of storage options work best for you. Do you need shelving, a table, hooks, pegboard? Then head to your local home-improvement store or hardware store and stock up on the necessary items.

The Least You Need to Know

♦ Practice proper piling to know what to keep, what to toss, and what to pass on to others.

♦ A broom (covered with a cloth or not) makes a great tool for sweeping down cobwebs from rafters and ceilings.

♦ That ancient-looking whatchamacallit you found in the attic may be worth big bucks! Bring it to an appraiser or an antique store.

♦ Mold is the mortal enemy of basements, so air out that space or dole out for a dehumidifier to keep the air dry.

Chapter 12

The Air We Breathe

In This Chapter

- Smokin': the furnace, fireplace, and other sources of fire
- Conditioning the air conditioner
- Cleaning air ducts
- Understanding potential allergens and your home
- Getting odors under control

Chemicals from cleaning products build up in the air of your home. Allergens like dust mites and pet dander float around. Cooking odors, smelly pets, and other pungent things annoy you and your family.

Don't breathe in dirty, smelly air—read on to find out how to keep the air in your home healthy and fresh smelling.

The Hot Stuff: Furnaces, Fireplaces, and More

Fire is probably one of the most important discoveries of mankind. Without fire, there would be no toasted marshmallows (and by extension, no s'mores), no cozy homes in December, no Fourth of July barbecues. But the cavemen who discovered fire used it outside and in well-ventilated caves. We're using it inside, where the by-products of combustion can be dangerous if they build up to certain levels. That's why it's important to have a method for venting these by-products.

Most heating systems have already thought of this for you; for example, the by-products from your fireplace go up the chimney, and your furnace has exhaust pipes and vents that carry the dangerous stuff outside the home. Have all your heating systems serviced at the beginning of every heating season by a professional to make sure these exhaust systems are in perfect working order.

Mary's Handy Hints

Change your CO detector batteries at the same time you change your fire alarm batteries—in the fall at daylight savings time. If your state doesn't do daylight savings time, mark your calendar to change the batteries every six months.

Smoky the Bear

Scary stuff: cigarette smoke can fill your home with about 40 types of carcinogens. Secondhand smoke is especially dangerous for children and people with lung or heart disease. The best remedy is—guess what?—to stop smoking. At the very least take your smoke breaks outside or near an open window. (See Chapter 9 for information on how to clean smoky walls.)

What You Don't Know *Can* Hurt You

One of the by-products of combustion is carbon monoxide (CO), which is a colorless, odorless, and poisonous gas. Relatively harmless in open spaces, CO can be deadly if allowed to accumulate. In fact, every year more people die of CO poisoning than from any other type of poisoning.

The best way to protect yourself and your family from this invisible hazard is with a CO detector. The U.S. Consumer Product Safety Commission recommends that every home have at least one CO detector with an audible alarm for each level of the home.

So Cool: Air Conditioners

Baby, it's hot outside! Whoever said that was so right ... in some parts of the country it's hot year round, whereas in others residents are hit with unbearable heat and humidity during the summer months. And then comes the familiar drone of ... the air conditioner. Savior of mankind!

The filter in your air conditioner traps particles and dirt so they don't go pouring back out into your home. Replace worn-out or otherwise yucky filters with a plastic electrostatic mesh filter from hardware stores or from RepairClinic.com. Just cut the filter to fit with a pair of scissors; the filter is made of polypropylene plastic mesh with an electrostatic charge that attracts particles from the air. To clean it, merely rinse it out, then let it dry before reinstalling it.

Getting the Dirt Out of Your Ducts

If your home heating system's ducts are dirty, your system can spew dust, dirt, and other gross stuff into your household air. Not only that, but dirt and debris are flammable and can spread fire. And if that isn't enough incentive to keep your ducts clean, consider this: dirty ducts can cause your heating bills to be higher than the national debt because the system won't work as efficiently.

Have your ducts cleaned by a professional every two to three years—more often if you smoke, have pets, or have a family member with breathing difficulties. A thorough cleaning can set you back up to $300, but your lungs will thank you.

What you can do on your own: every so often, vacuum the return air duct after removing the register grill, or use a broom to whisk away debris.

Airing Out Your Home

Many homes these days are built with great insulation that keeps the house warm in the winter and cool in the summer. The bad news is that the same insulation that keeps the heat and coolness indoors also keeps in all the pollutants that can be harmful to your health and your house. Old, drafty houses have an advantage after all!

Here are some of the things that can be trapped in your house that proper ventilation can help resolve:

- **Moisture.** Home and health enemies such as mold, mildew, bacteria, dust mites, dry rot, and insects thrive on moisture.

> **Mary's Handy Hints**
>
> Burn 100 percent soy candles. Soy candles emit very little if any smoke, and they do not contain the lead wicks that are so toxic to breathe. Plus they burn four to five times longer than regular wax candles with a gentle, not overpowering, scent.

- **Cigarette smoke.** We all know by now the harmful effects of cigarette smoke, both firsthand and secondhand!

- **Combustion products.** Carbon monoxide, carbon dioxide, soot, and other goodies are produced by fuel-burning heating equipment, gas water heaters, fireplaces, woodstoves, gas ranges, and even candles.

- **Heat.** Sun exposure can cause overheating in the attic.

- **Particles.** They're invisible to the naked eye, but we wish they would disappear forever: dust and dust mites, pet dander, pollen, lead, and asbestos.

- **Common household chemicals.** As mentioned in Chapter 3, cleaning products emit chemical residues in your home. Add the fumes from paints, solvents, pesticides, odors and formaldehyde from furniture, carpet, and building materials, and you have quite the nasty trappings.

Now that you know what you want to move … how do you move it? The best way to move the air through your home is by opening the windows on opposite sides of the house. This will pull the breeze through your house. (Just be sure to keep the interior doors between the two windows open!)

If there is no breeze to take advantage of, open the lowest (such as a low downstairs window) and highest (such as a skylight or upstairs window) windows in your home to create a "chimney effect" that pulls air through the house.

You can increase the effect of either method with reversible window fans. Set the one on the side where the breeze in coming in to push air into the house, and set the one on the other side to suck the air out.

Ah-choo! Allergies and You

If you find people saying "Gezundheit" to you more than anything else, you may have allergies. The causes may be dust mite excretions (how appetizing!), pollen, pet dander—tiny flakes of skin that float in the air—or any number of other pollutants in your home.

Of course, you should see your doctor for the appropriate tests and treatment. But cleaning the air in your home goes a long way toward easing your symptoms. Try these tips:

- ◆ Bathe your pet frequently. Even cats can get used to this!

- ◆ Buy a vacuum with a high-efficiency particulate air (HEPA) filter, which traps small particles and prevents them from spewing out the back of the machine.

- ◆ Purchase a HEPA air cleaning machine for your bedroom.

- ◆ Vacuum and dust your home frequently; if you're the one who's allergic, wear a dust mask while you do this work.

- ◆ Reduce or eliminate dust-holding furnishings such as upholstered furniture, drapes, and rugs. Hey, the simple look is in!

Remember, ventilate, ventilate, ventilate. Trapping yourself inside a weather-tight home with pet dander, dust, mold, and other allergens worsens allergic reactions. If you are allergic to tree or other outdoor pollen where opening a window only worsens your symptoms, then a whole-house air purifier might be your solution.

Dirty Words

A word of warning: whole house purifiers can be very pricy! You need to hire a specialist to install it as well. But if that's what keeps your allergies at bay, it may be worth it!

PU: Odor Control

Do visitors wrinkle their noses when they enter your abode? Do skunks flee in terror from your yard? Do people refer to your home as "that smelly house on Main Street"? Fear not—here are some ways to banish offensive odors in your home.

To permanently rid your home of odor, you must locate the source and rectify the problem. The suggestions that follow are temporary fixes only.

Cooking Smells

Fish for dinner? You may want to do something to eliminate the odor from the air once you're done cooking. While you're doing the dishes, lightly simmer ¼ cup of white vinegar (yes, there we go again with the vinegar) in 2 cups of water for 5 to 10 minutes. That should absorb most of the odors. You can also take a spray bottle that has a fine mist spray, add a teaspoon of white vinegar, fill it with water, and spritz the air.

Fridges, Closets, and Other Enclosed Spaces

If your fridge smells funky and your closet reeks of old socks, try these remedies:

 ♦ **Charcoal.** Activated charcoal (like the kind used in fish aquariums) will absorb most offensive odors. Place it in a dish on the floor or on a shelf, or hang it in a mesh bag.

 ♦ **Baking soda.** Step 1: Open container of baking soda. Step 2: Place in smelly location. Step 3: Change every three months or so. What could be easier?

Smells from Fido and Fluffy

Pets have body odor, just like humans—but unlike humans, they can't just slather on some Arrid Xtra Dry and be done with it (or they can't put their Right Guard under their left arm). They also have cages and litter boxes indoors, and these add to the smell snafus. Follow these tips to keep your home smelling fresh:

◆ Wash and groom your pets frequently.

◆ Clean out your pets' cages and cat boxes often, preferably out-doors.

◆ Make sure your home is well ventilated. (There's that *V* word again!)

◆ Keep pets' cages and litter boxes in a well-ventilated space and away from the living area.

◆ Shampoo carpets and upholstery more frequently than you might need to if you didn't have pets.

These tips work great for most pet odors, but what about when kitty has an "accident" outside his litter box? Unneutered males spray urine to mark their territory, and even neutered males may occasion-ally do this. Cats may also urinate outside the box for medical or behavioral reasons. And dogs aren't immune to this type of behavior—they may wet on the floor if they're feeling anxious.

Mary's Handy Hints

If your pet's odor problem is a little smellier—for ex-ample, he encountered a skunk—forget the tomato juice method, and head to the pet supply store or your vet for a commercial odor-removing product.

If your cat urinates outside the box, you need to remove the odor entirely, or he'll come to see the place as a favorite spot to go again and again. And of course, you'll want to remove the smell from Fido's accident as well. We've had luck with blotting up the urine and then cleaning the spot with a water and white vinegar solution. You can also buy a commercial enzyme-cleaning product at the pet supply store.

Enzyme products must be used before any other product, including vinegar. Other products will "kill" the enzymes, preventing them from "eating" the bacteria causing the odor. On carpets, always treat an area twice as large as the surface stain. Urine hits the padding and spreads.

The Least You Need to Know

- All heating systems that use fire can cause dangerous carbon monoxide (CO) to build up in your home. Invest in a CO detector for each level of your home.

- Ventilation helps rid your home of air pollutants from household chemical residues to pet dander.

- Rid your home of odors with baking soda, activated charcoal, enzyme-cleaning products, and vinegar.

- Pets and dust mites in your home can cause allergies. If you or anyone in your family has allergies, be extra vigilant about keeping your home clean.

Part 4

Other Cleaning Challenges

In this part, we strive to make doing the laundry easier and quicker. We tell you how to read fabric care labels (and when to ignore them), how to choose a water temperature and a cycle, and even how to remove dozens of stains from your clothing (not that you have dozens of stains on your clothing—not all at once, anyway!).

Are you always in a rush or too impatient to spend hours cleaning your home? We also show you how to make short work of housework. We even have a whole-house cleaning plan that you can whip through in an hour! Finally, we share the secrets of cleaning electronic gadgets such as cameras, computers, DVD players, and more. (Hint: Do not put these items in the dishwasher.)

Chapter 13

Laundry Basics

In This Chapter

- Whitening whites and brightening brights
- Deciphering the laundry cycles
- Cleaning labels—their symbolic logic
- Learning the ABCs of stain removal

It piles up on floors, it threatens to take over the bathroom. It looks bad and smells worse. A swamp monster from a horror film? Hardly—it's your dirty laundry. In fact, back in the days when Monday was the traditional laundry day, it was such an onerous task that the day was labeled "Blue Monday."

Not only is dirty laundry scary to contemplate, it's also confusing. Do light clothes go with the whites or the colors? What temperature water works best? What do all those crazy symbols on the cleaning labels mean?

We're here to make doing the laundry easy for you (or at least as easy as it can get).

Sorting Clothes

Sorting is the practice of separating clothing into piles with similar characteristics—such as color and delicateness—so that they can receive similar treatments. If you didn't sort clothing, you'd either have to wash one item at a time (and devote your entire life to doing the laundry) or be happy wearing shrunken sweaters and newly pink T-shirts.

After you've gathered a good-size pile of laundry to be washed, sort it according to these characteristics, and in this order:

1. **Washing method.** Different fabrics and types of clothing require different washing methods—hand washing, gentle cycle, permanent press, and so on. You should now have several piles sorted.

2. **Color.** Now sort each of the washing piles according to its color. The basic groupings are white, light, medium, and dark. Here are some specifics:

   White: white (of course), very pale yellow, or beige.

   Light: powder blue, light tan, light grey, misty green.

Mary's Handy Hints

Anything with red shading should be washed together, including red, dark pink, and purple.

Medium: sky blue, mint green, tan, grey, yellow, khaki, camel, light pink (test for colorfastness first).

Dark: navy blue, brown, blue jeans, green and dark green, charcoal grey, medium pink (test it first for colorfastness).

3. **Amount or type of soil.** Out of each pile, separate the clothing that's muddy, greasy, or otherwise heavily soiled. This way, you won't wash a barely soiled blouse with greasy rags and end up with a greasy blouse.

4. **The dangerousness of the clothing.** This is our highly amusing way of saying that the article of clothing will cause other clothes to snag, gather lint, absorb dye, and so on. This depends on the mix of clothes in the pile; for example, a zipper may damage your nylons, but not your jeans.

If you follow these sorting directions and end up with 50 little piles of laundry, you can make some smart compromises. For example, you can wash very light items with white items. Or you can wash clothes that can take a heavy washing (such as jeans) in with clothes destined for the gentle cycle (assuming the clothes are not very dirty).

Deciphering Cleaning Labels

Look at the cleaning instructions label on your new slacks, and what do you see? No, not the words "Permanent press wash, only nonchlorine bleach when needed, tumble dry normal." What you see is a jumble of symbols that would make hieroglyphics experts blanch in terror.

Here is a guide to those symbols, so you can wash your clothes with confidence—and without an advanced degree in symbolic logic.

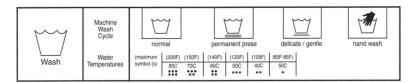

Washing cycles and temperatures.

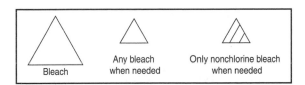

Bleach and nonchlorine bleach.

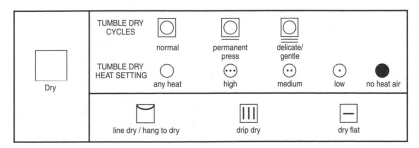

Dryer cycles and settings.

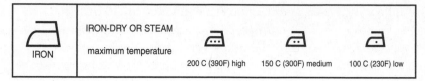

Iron or steam settings.

Knowing what not to do.

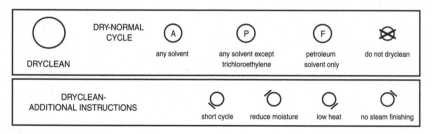

Dry cleaning information.

Additional garment instructions.

When to Ignore Care Labels

Ignore care labels? Gasp! All those teachers who told you to carefully follow directions would get the vapors if they knew you were doing this. But sometimes you can get away with flouting the rules.

For example, if you're very familiar with the fabric and construction of a garment, you may know that you can treat it in ways other than those suggested on the care label. A label may, for instance, have no instructions for ironing, which means that the item generally doesn't need ironing to maintain its look; however, this doesn't mean you *can't* iron it. In fact, you can iron away with abandon. Also, you can usually treat an item of clothing more carefully than the label suggests. For example, if the label recommends a warm water wash, this means that you shouldn't use hot; but it doesn't mean that you can't wash it in cold water occasionally if it's more convenient for you.

When Not to Ignore Care Labels

Most often, though, it pays to play it safe. You should always follow the directions on care labels if:

- The label contains detailed instructions. This indicates that the instructions are important to follow.

- The garment is very expensive and difficult to replace.

- You have other clothing by this manufacturer and have found its instructions to be reliable.

- The garment is a specialty item with flocking, fur, or another unusual construction.

In other words, err on the side of caution when dealing with your washing. You can ignore care labels by being more careful than the label suggests, but you should always follow the instructions on clothes that have unusual detailing or construction.

Choosing a Water Temperature

Your goal is to choose the hottest water the fabric will bear without fading, shrinking to the size of Barbie doll clothing, or otherwise becoming damaged.

Laundry soaps work best in hot water. Hot water also kills microorganisms and sanitizes better than warm or cold; however, warm and cold water keep colors brighter, minimize shrinking and fading, and are better for removing protein stains such as blood.

Here's how you can break down cold, warm, and hot water for laundering:

♦ Cold water is 80°F (26.7°C for you metric folks) or colder. Use cold water for delicate items, clothing that is lightly soiled, protein stains such as blood, garments with dyes that may bleed or run, and for the final rinse of the wash cycle.

♦ Warm water is 90°F to 100°F (32.2°C to 43.3°C). Go warm for permanent press, colorfast brights, and dark colors.

♦ Hot water is 130°F (54.4°C) or above. Because it sanitizes better than warm or cold, you should use hot water on the following:

Sheets and pillowcases

Bath and hand towels

Cleaning rags

Fabrics soiled with oily dirt

Dish towels and dish rags

Diapers (not the disposable kind, thank you very much)

Heavily soiled work and play clothes

Sturdy whites, lights, and pastel prints

Unless you have a washing machine that heats its own water, the hot water in your machine is only as hot as the temperature you have set on your water heater. Further, the water cools a bit as the washer fills and even more by the time the wash cycle has finished.

Deciphering Wash Cycles

Regular, *permanent press*, delicate ... figuring out which wash cycle to use can be pretty confusing. Who even knows what permanent press means? Here's the lowdown on the cycles.

The Regular Cycle

Use an all-purpose or heavy-duty detergent in the long, hot regular wash cycle. Sturdy cottons, linens, and heavily soiled clothes should be washed in the regular cycle. Presoak any heavily soiled clothing.

Tidy Terms

Permanent press refers to a fabric that's been chemically processed to resist wrinkles and hold its shape.

The Permanent Press Cycle

Wash synthetic fibers other than acrylic, modacrylic, acetate, and rayon (which require hand washing or the gentle cycle) on the permanent press cycle. Shorter than the regular cycle, the permanent press cycle provides a cool-down rinse and a cold final rinse plus a slower spin speed to prevent wrinkles from setting into synthetic fabrics. All-purpose detergents are fine for this cycle.

The Gentle or Delicate Cycle

Use the gentle or delicate cycle for washable lace, lingerie, nylons, and other clothing that indicates gentle treatment on the care label. This cycle has a short, slow agitation cycle, cool to warm water, and a cold rinse. Use a mild detergent for this cycle.

Whitening Whites

Do your white clothes appear dingy even though you bleach them? Believe it or not, bleach can cause the discoloration. Add ½ to 1 cup of 20 percent hydrogen peroxide or 2 to 3 cups of 3 percent hydrogen

Dirty Words

Never use hydrogen peroxide or bleach on silk, wool, or dry-clean-only clothing. Do not use chlorine bleach on baby clothing; it can irritate babies' skin.

peroxide per regular washer. The first time you do this, allow the clothes to soak in the washer for 30 minutes. Then wash normally, only using less detergent. White clothes return to their normal brightness and colored clothes perk up as well.

Drying Your Clothes

Congratulations! Your clothes are now clean. But they're also wet, and people will laugh at you if you wear your clothes out on the street without drying them first.

So what should and, most importantly, *shouldn't* actually go into the dryer? Most machine washable items can be dried in the dryer. But the exceptions are as follows:

- Rubber
- Fiberglass
- Acetate, acrylic, and spandex
- Drip-dry clothing
- Plastic
- Delicate fibers such as viscose rayon
- Wools other than Superwash and other treated wools
- Microfiber

> **Mary's Handy Hints**
>
> Fill your dryer about one third full, because clothes will fluff up as they dry. Overfilling can lead to wrinkling, linting, and other ugly snafus.

Just as with washing your clothes, the temperature you choose for your dryer cycle can make the difference between nicely finished clothing and Barbie-size clothing. Here are your options:

- **Regular.** Regular is the hottest temperature setting, and is best for sturdy cottons such as T-shirts, towels, and preshrunk jeans.

- ◆ **Medium.** The medium setting is for permanent press
  clothing, wrinkle-treated
  clothing, many synthetics, some
  knits, and lightweight cottons
  and linens.

- ◆ **Low.** The low or delicate setting is for cotton knits, lingerie,
  and sheer fabrics.

Follow the instructions on the care
label, which will tell you whether or
not the garment can be dried and, if
so, which temperature setting to use.

Dirty Words

And you thought we
were all finished. Not so!
Sorting is important for drying
clothes, too! Don't mix non-
colorfast items with white or
light loads, or the colors may
bleed onto your light clothing.
Also sort according by fabric
weight, because lightweight
items dry more quickly than
heavier garments.

Stain Removal 101

The basic rule for stain removal: Give Your Product Time to Work.
Apply the cleaner we suggest below for the type of stain you're dealing
with and allow it to set undisturbed for at least 15 minutes. (Silk, wool,
and dry-clean-only clothes are best left to a professional garment cleaning company.)

Clean spills immediately. The longer a stain sets, the more stubborn it
becomes. Use a clean white rag to remove a stain, because the color
from the rag could transfer to the fabric or surface you are cleaning.
Apply the cleaner to the rag and blot on the stain.

When working with fabrics, always blot—never rub. Rubbing breaks
down the fibers and weakens the material. After 15 minutes, blot to
remove the stain. Reapply the cleaner rather than attempting to rub out
the stain. Move the rag each time
you blot to prevent spreading the
stain.

After removing the stain, rinse with
vinegar and water (¼ cup per quart
of water) followed by plain water.
Use cool water to treat a stain; heat
of any kind sets a stain.

Dirty Words

The guidelines here may
not apply to every fabric or
surface. Before using a cleaner
on any fabric or surface, test
an inconspicuous spot first for
colorfastness.

Wash the garment after removing the stain, then air dry. Dryer heat permanently sets the stain if it's not entirely removed.

Removing Stains from Dry-Clean-Only Clothes

Dry-clean-only clothing including silk and wool sometimes can be treated with a dry-cleaning solvent, although often these solvents stain the clothing. Dry-cleaning solvents can also be expensive. A less-expensive way to go is cleaner used for vehicle brakes called Brake Cleaner—do not confuse with brake fluid. It is the same solvent.

Foaming shaving cream is another excellent product to remove many stains and may be safe to use on some dry-clean-only clothes. Spray a bit of the shaving cream on the stain. The shaving cream works best if left alone; it does not need your help at this point. Wait 15 minutes, blot, then rinse as previously instructed. Always test a small, inconspicuous spot first before treating anything—even with cold water.

Removing Stains from Leather and Vinyl Clothing

Leather and vinyl cleaners and conditioners will remove a few stains such as ink and nonoily food stains. It is best to have leather and vinyl clothing cleaned by a professional dry cleaner who is knowledgeable with leather and vinyl care. Call a leather shop for recommendations. Keep leather and vinyl clothing conditioned and cleaned regularly to prevent drying and cracking.

Your Stain Removal Dictionary

Here's how to remove just about any type of stain you can think of, from adhesives to wax.

- ◆ **Adhesive.** *See* Glue and adhesive.
- ◆ **Baby formula.** Hydrogen peroxide removes the yellowing in christening gowns. Mix a 50/50 solution of a 3 percent peroxide and water. Soak for 30 minutes and launder as normal. Air dry. Pour peroxide directly on a formula stain. Wait 30 to 60 minutes adding more peroxide if the stain has not disappeared. Launder in cold water. Adding a bit of baking soda to the peroxide often helps "bubble" out the stain.

◆ **Ballpoint ink.** Follow the "Stain Removal 101" guidelines. Dip a Q-Tip in straight rubbing alcohol and gently blot on the ink mark. Wait 30 minutes. If any ink remains, reapply the alcohol and let it set another 30 to 60 minutes. Keep the spot damp with the alcohol. Rinse with cool water and white vinegar. The Q-Tip keeps the alcohol confined to the area of the ink, which helps prevent the ink from spreading further on the clothing. We do not recommend using hairspray for ink removal. The alcohol in hairspray removes the ink but the other chemicals in hairspray could damage a fabric.

Dirty Words

Gel ink pens should always be used for writing checks to avoid a check from being acid washed and rewritten. So it makes sense that gel ink is difficult to remove. Keep the lid on the pen and use all caution when using the pen around fabric. Keep these and magic markers well out of the reach of little ones.

◆ **Beer and alcohol.** For all fabrics other than silk, wool, or linen: immediately rinse with cool water, then blot with a clean white towel. Then pour an enzyme product such as Bac Out or Nature's Miracle onto the spot. Let that set 30 to 60 minutes, adding more enzyme product if needed. Launder in cool water and air dry. If you are in a restaurant, dab on a bit of liquid hand soap from the restroom. Wait a few minutes and rinse with cool water. Soak the stain in cool sudsy water when you return home. Launder in cool water and air dry.

◆ **Berry stains.** These aren't as difficult to remove as you think. Pour 3 percent hydrogen peroxide on the stain and let it set 30 to 60 minutes. Then dab on liquid dishwashing detergent or make a paste of borax and water and paste on the stain. Let that set overnight and launder as usual. Air dry.

◆ **Blood.** Follow the "Stain Removal 101" guidelines. Flush the garment immediately with cool water. Then soak in cool water for 5 minutes. Rinse and treat with an enzyme product such as Bac Out or Nature's Miracle. Wait 30 to 60 minutes, then launder in cool water and air dry. To remove bloodstains that do not respond to the enzymes, old bloodstains, or if the garment has gone through the dryer: soak the stain in straight 3 percent hydrogen peroxide.

Do not use regular household bleach. Rinse with a vinegar-and-water solution and again in cool water. Air dry. Always test a spot first for colorfastness.

♦ **Chocolate and cooking oil.** Immediately dab on liquid dish-washing soap and wait 30 to 60 minutes. Rinse and repeat if needed. Use foaming shaving cream if some of the stain still remains. Wait 15 minutes then rinse.

♦ **Coffee or Coke.** Spray on Ion-A-Clean or use 3 percent hydrogen peroxide. Wait 45 seconds and blot to remove. Repeat if needed. Foaming shaving cream also does a good job removing coffee or Coke stains, as does a paste made with borax and white vinegar. Rinse with cool water, and then launder and air dry.

♦ **Crayon.** Lay the cloth on a clean, white paper towel with a piece of plastic underneath the towel. Use a Q-Tip to dab a bit of DeSolvIt on the spot. (Always test a small, inconspicuous spot before using DeSolvIt.) Wait 30 minutes and gently blot. Check the towel every 10 minutes and reshift the towel when the crayon has soaked onto the towel, as the crayon stain may soak right through the stained fabric. Repeat after 30 minutes if needed. This time, wash the clothing in warm water and air dry.

♦ **Deodorant.** Soak the garment in hot water for several minutes. Then treat as a perspiration stain (*see* Perspiration).

♦ **Dirt.** Follow the "Stain Removal 101" guidelines. Spray on Ion-A-Clean and leave it alone for 45 to 60 seconds. Or dab on a bit of liquid dishwashing soap and allow to set several hours even overnight. Blot, then rinse with vinegar and water or machine wash immediately. Foaming shaving cream also does a good job removing stubborn dirt or dirt that has gone through the dryer.

 Dirty Words _____

We speak sometimes of using a concentrated orange cleaner to remove oil and grease, but make sure it does not contain petroleum distillates. Companies are getting tricky as to how they list the distillates—they may be called mineral spirits or aliphatic hydrocarbon or just carbon. Look for the "Caution" warning. If the bottle contains that warning, it may also contain a distillate, which can stain your clothing.

◆ **Dye.** Read the "Stain Removal 101" guidelines. Red dye is found in punch, Popsicles, Kool-Aid, and candles that are red or purple in color. Red or purple dyes are best removed with hydrogen peroxide. Regular household bleach in most cases only makes the stain worse. Remember to always test an inconspicuous spot first for colorfastness. Use 3 percent peroxide and blot onto the stain. Be sure to protect working surfaces. Wait 30 minutes, rinse with ⅓ cup of white vinegar per quart of water, and then again with plain water. Repeat if needed.

◆ **Feces.** Feces are best removed with an enzyme product such as Bac Out or Nature's Miracle. The enzymes neutralize the odors and remove the stains. Pour on and saturate the area. Follow the bottle directions. Blot to remove. Rinse with plain water and dry. Repeat if needed. Do not use a cleaner before applying an enzyme product. The cleaner will kill the enzymes, rendering them useless. Most cleaners will not remove the odor. Odors are caused by the bacteria, which grow and multiply, causing the odor to worsen with time. Enzymes are most affective for removing odors.

◆ **Food.** Food never spills down your front unless you are out in public where it quickly makes a mockery of your front side. Should that happen, ask the waitress for a glass of club soda. Gently dab a bit on the clothing and resist the temptation to rub. It may look funny until you get home, but the food stain comes right out. For greasy fried food or gravy-type stains, head to the restroom and dab on a bit of liquid hand soap. Wait a few minutes then blot with a cool damp cloth. At home, immediately blot the spot with an enzyme product such as Nature's Miracle or Bac Out. Wait an hour and repeat if needed. If the stain is stubbornly refusing to budge, gently rub in a bit of liquid dishwashing soap and leave it overnight. Launder the next day in cool water. Alternatively, you can spray the spot with foaming shaving cream. Resist the temptation to play in the foam. The shaving cream doesn't need any help at all. Wait 15 minutes, blot, and rinse with vinegar and water.

◆ **Glue and adhesive.** Follow the "Stain Removal 101" guidelines for making certain to protect the work surface. Glue and adhesive requires a concentrated orange cleaner or an acid-based product to dissolve the sticky residue. DeSolvIt works quite well. Products such as Goo Gone or Goop Off also work for glue and adhesive but can stain clothing. Always test an inconspicuous spot first. Wipe off what you can with a clean white cloth. Blot on the cleaner. Wait for an hour, then blot to remove. Do not rub to remove, and reapply the cleaner if necessary. Then apply liquid dishwashing soap to remove the cleaner, and rinse with vinegar and water. School glue such as Elmer's generally rinses off after a long soaking in cold water. Foaming shaving cream often removes other types of glue (such as what is used for crafts).

◆ **Grass stains.** Immediately rub in a bit of a concentrated cleaner such as Bi-O-Kleen or Bio Ox. Liquid dishwashing soaps also do a good job removing grass stains. Let the cleaner set overnight, then gently rub, and then rinse with cool water and wash. Air dry the garment to make sure the stain has been completely removed.

◆ **Grease and oil.** *See Glue and adhesive.*

Mary's Handy Hints

When working with stained clothing, always put a piece of plastic between layers of clothing to prevent the stain from soaking onto the second layer. Put a clean but old towel on your work surface to protect the surface.

◆ **Gum.** Freeze the gum with a cube of ice, scraping off what you can with a scraper. Repeat until most of the gum has been removed. If you have room in your freezer, you can freeze the clothing as well to freeze the gum. Anything remaining can be removed by applying DeSolvIt, and then dab on liquid dishwashing soap to remove the cleaner and rinse with vinegar and water.

◆ **Hair dye.** Good luck!

◆ **Hand lotion.** Gently rub in foaming shaving cream. Wait 30 minutes and rinse with cool water.

◆ **Iodine.** Follow the "Stain Removal 101" guidelines. Treat immediately. The longer it sets, the harder it is to remove this stain. After rinsing in cool water, pour on 3 percent hydrogen peroxide. Wait 15 minutes and repeat. Wait 60 minutes. If the stain still remains, it's permanent. Iodine is very difficult to remove. You can try soaking it overnight with a paste made from peroxide and borax.

♦ **Juice.** *See Kool-Aid.*

♦ **Kool-Aid, popsicles, punch, and grape juice.** These stains are all caused by red dye 40 except for grape juice, but they are treated the same way. Immediately pour 3 percent peroxide on the spot and let it set for 30 minutes. Rinse in cool water and repeat if needed. Launder in cool water and air dry.

♦ **Lipstick.** Follow the "Stain Removal 101" guidelines. Dampen with cool water, then rub on liquid dishwashing detergent. After an hour, rinse with cool water. That should remove most of the lipstick. Repeat if necessary. Then soak with straight hydrogen peroxide to remove any stain. A concentrated cleaner such as Bio Ox or Bi-O-Clean will also remove lipstick. Make sure it does not contain petroleum distillates or limonene. If the clothing has gone through the dryer, the stain is probably permanent. At this point try using straight hydrogen peroxide to remove any color. Peroxide won't remove the lipstick, only the stain that remains.

♦ **Magic marker.** When the label reads permanent, that means permanent. Sometimes repeated cleaning with a concentrated cleaner or liquid dishwashing soap helps remove the stain. Dab on and let it set overnight. Do not dry the garment until the stain is completely gone.

♦ **Makeup.** If the makeup is on the collar of a blouse, shirt, or jacket, saturate the collar with a diluted concentrated cleaner such as Bio Ox or Bi-O-Kleen. If the stain has not completely soaked out of the collar, blot on a bit of hair shampoo before laundering. Do not rinse. Then launder the next day as normal in cool water. Spraying the area with 3 percent hydrogen peroxide also helps to remove the stain. Air dry.

♦ **Mascara.** Remove mascara with petroleum jelly. Gently rub on and let it set 15 to 30 minutes. Mineral spirits also removes water-proof mascara. Rinse with soapy water and launder. Mineral spirits and petroleum jelly are both petroleum products. Test a small area first.

- **Merthiolate.** *See Iodine.*

- **Milk.** Immediately pour an enzyme product such as Bac Out or Nature's Miracle onto the spot. Wait 60 minutes, then rinse with cool water.

- **Mold/mildew.** Musty-smelling clothes can be hung in the sun to air out. If the clothes are colorfast, fill the washer with cool water, add 2 cups of hydrogen peroxide, and allow to set 30 minutes. Wash and air dry in the sun. Heat will set the smell of mold, so air dry to make certain the mold has been completely killed.

- **Mustard.** Follow the directions for *Coffee and Coke.* An enzyme product such as Bac Out and Nature's Miracle also works on ornery mustard stains.

- **Nail polish.** Follow the "Stain Removal 101" guidelines. Use a nonacetone fingernail polish remover. Dab on, wait 30 minutes, and rinse with vinegar and water. If the acetone fails to remove the polish, try some dry-cleaning solvent. After the stain has been removed, dab on some liquid dishwashing soap, wait 10 minutes, and then rinse. Always test a small spot first before using dry-cleaning solvents.

> ### Cleaning Quips
>
> "I hate housework! You make the beds, you do the dishes—and six months later you have to start all over again."
>
> —Joan Rivers

- **Paint (latex, water-based paints and art paint).** Turpentine removes paint stains from most surfaces. Do remember that turpentine is difficult to remove from clothing and can spontaneously combust on a cloth of any kind. Blot on and wait 30 minutes to an hour. Blot and repeat. Soak in sudsy water for several hours, and then rinse with a vinegar and water solution. If turpentine does not remove latex house paint, dampen the fabric and then apply foaming shaving cream. Wait 24 hours, then rinse. It does work! Foaming shaving cream has also been known to remove art paint.

- **Perspiration stains.** These remove easily by pouring 3 percent peroxide directly onto the underarm area. Wait 60 minutes and launder as usual. Always test a small spot first for colorfastness.

- **Petroleum jelly.** Follow the "Stain Removal 101" guidelines. Remove petroleum jelly immediately. It is an oil-based product; and the longer it sets, the more likely it will leave a permanent discoloration. Blot and apply liquid dishwashing soap, and then wait 30 minutes to an hour. Rinse and repeat if necessary.

- **Popsicles and punch.** *See Kool-Aid.*

- **Rust.** Squeeze enough juice from a fresh lemon to thoroughly saturate the spot. Generously sprinkle on some salt and let that set 24 hours. Refresh the lemon juice several times during the day. Rinse with cool water and repeat if needed.

- **Sap.** Peanut butter often removes tree sap. Dab on a good bit of it, giving it an hour to loosen the sap. Repeat if needed. If that doesn't work, then use DeSolvIt following the stain-removal guidelines.

- **Scorch marks.** Scorch marks made by irons or burns are not removable. They are burned into the fabric.

- **Shoe polish.** First apply 3 percent hydrogen peroxide to the spot. Wait 30 to 60 minutes and repeat if the polish is lightening. If that does not reduce the color, mix a paste of borax and peroxide directly on the spot. The bubbling action of the peroxide and borax sometimes adds enough agitation to lift the stain. Remember, shoe polish is generally permanent and can be very difficult to remove. Prevention is wise when applying polish.

- **Suntan lotion.** Blot by placing a white paper towel on both the top and bottom of the fabric. Continuously move the towels as you blot, being careful not to spread the lotion to other areas of the fabric. This can be done by folding the towel into quarters, then using the top and bottom sides of the towel. Change to fresh towels if necessary. Next, apply hair shampoo to the spot, work it in, and let it set an hour. Wash immediately in hot water.

- **Tar.** *See Glue and adhesive.*

- **Urine.** Generally, rinsing immediately in sudsy water and adding ½ cup of vinegar and ¼ cup of baking soda removes urine stains and odors in clothing. Rinse and air dry to make certain you completely removed the stain.

◆ **Wax.** Freeze the wax with ice. If you have freezer space, place the garment in the freezer. The wax hardens and chips off immediately. To remove any remaining wax, place the garment on top of a paper towel or a paper bag containing no printing. Then put an all white paper towel on top of the wax. Set the iron to medium and iron over the wax. The iron melts the wax into the paper bag or towel. If you use a paper towel or bag with printing, the heat from the iron sets the ink into the fabric. And who wants to walk around with "Stop & Shop" imprinted onto their favorite shirt? If the wax has color, do not use the iron. The heat will set the dye into the fabric. Instead, after removing (or freezing off) the wax, saturate the spot with 3 percent hydrogen peroxide. Wait 30 to 60 minutes and rinse.

> **Mary's Handy Hints**
>
> Got a stain that just won't come out? As a last resort, try saturating it with 3 percent peroxide for 30 minutes. It might surprise you and come out, even after going through the dryer.

◆ **Yellowing.** Antique lace and tablecloths yellow with age. Fill a sink with cool water, adding 1 cup of 3 percent hydrogen peroxide. Do not use chlorine bleach because it worsens the yellowing. Soak the item for 30 minutes. If the yellow has not disappeared, add 1 more cup more of peroxide and soak another 30 minutes. Rinse in a mixture of ⅓ cup of vinegar to 1 gallon of water. Air dry. Should your clothes begin to appear yellow or gray, chances are you have been using regular household bleach. Chlorine bleach will turn the whitest of whites a dingy color after repeated launderings. To brighten them, fill the washer with cool water and add 2 cups of 3 percent hydrogen peroxide or ½ cup of 20 percent peroxide and half the normal amount of detergent. Add the clothes and allow them to soak for 30 minutes. Continue the wash cycle. If after 30 minutes the clothes still appear yellow, add more peroxide to the water and continue soaking for another 30 minutes.

This guide should help you keep your clothing clean and stain-free. If you're worried about stains on any other item, from leather to carpet to wood floors, check out Appendix A.

Mary's Handy Hints

Enzyme stain removers such as Bac Out and Nature's Miracle do wonders removing bacteria-based stains caused by food, fecal matter, urine, and tannin stains (such as red wine). The enzymes "eat" away the bacteria, which gets rid of the odor and the stain. They do not work if another cleaner has been previously used. The cleaner will kill the enzymes, so use it as a first resource and not the last.

The Least You Need to Know

◆ Knowing how to sort clothes is key to getting your clothes their cleanest.

◆ Believe it or not, you can sometimes ignore the care label instructions on fabrics.

◆ Match up your wash cycle, water temperature, and detergent for the best results.

◆ Sort your clothes for the dryer and choose the temperature setting suggested on the item's care label.

◆ Having the right products on hand—such as 3 percent hydrogen peroxide, foaming shaving cream, and an enzyme cleaner—will go a long way toward keeping your clothing stain-free.

Chapter 14

Electronic Gadgets

In This Chapter

- Cleaning up the TV, VCR, and DVD player
- Prettying your picture-perfect cameras
- Cleaning those CDs and CD players
- Making sure the computer comes clean

Did you ever see the movie *The Matrix*, where machines take over the world? In the movie, everything we humans experience is a computer program that's fed into our brains as the world-dominating machines use us as an energy source.

Our theory is that the machines started out as nice, docile TVs, DVD players, and computers that were abused by their humans. We spilled Coke on their keyboards, let our kids stick Goldfish Crackers into their slots, and kicked them when they stopped working perfectly. These formerly nice machines rose up and took over the world!

Don't let this happen in real life—treat your electronic equipment kindly and clean it regularly, and it will serve you for years to come.

In this chapter, we'll tell you how to give your electronic equipment—from cameras to computers—tender loving care.

Clean Enough for Daytime TV

We can do little about the dirt that spews at us from inside the TV. We can, however, keep tabs on the layers of dust and grime that land on the screen, buttons, casing, and remote control on the outside of the TV.

Cleaning up TV is easy with these tips:

♦ Any dust floating within a 50-foot radius of the TV can't help but be drawn to the TV screen by its unrelenting magnetism. Dust your television screen every week with an electrostatic dust cloth. These cloths are designed to attract and hold dust. Toss them in the laundry like you do ordinary cloths.

♦ After you've whisked away the dust from a standard tube or plasma-screen TV, clean it with a damp cloth. Spray a bit of rubbing alcohol on a soft cloth such as an old but clean cotton T-shirt and wipe the screen, avoiding the ventilation slots. Dry immediately with a soft cloth. LCD (liquid crystal display) TVs and DLP (digital light processing) screens should never be cleaned with a damp cloth. Dust them with only a soft, dry, clean cotton cloth such as a T-shirt. Do not use terrycloth or microfiber cloths on these screens. Consult your owner's manual before cleaning a TV screen, or use the cleaning kit if one came with your TV.

Dirty Words

You may have read that you can clean TV screens with fabric softener sheets. Don't! The chemicals in these sheets will deteriorate the surface of the screen over time.

♦ Clean the knobs and buttons by dusting them with a clean, dry paintbrush or a new, clean pastry brush. Wipe the casing with a dry cloth or lightly spritz a cloth with a solution of one part baby shampoo to three parts water. The cleaner must be a neutral pH. If sticky fingers have gummed up the knobs, lightly spray a very small amount of cleaner on a soft cotton cloth, using caution to prevent the cleaner from seeping into the controls.

Dust in the air? In your home? You better believe it. See Chapter 13 for tips about reducing dust in your home.

Fast-Forwarding to Clean: The VCR

You can easily keep the VCR clean—just stick to G-rated movies. (We suggest *The Lion King*.) As for the outside and internal components of the VCR, follow these tips:

◆ Start by reading the owner's manual, which will give you specific instructions for cleaning your VCR.

◆ Have one of those old-school VCRs with the wooden casing? Clean it with furniture polish, spraying it onto a cloth (not directly onto the VCR).

◆ Clean the knobs, buttons, and exterior as we instructed for TVs.

◆ Clean the tape heads of a VCR about once every two months, depending on how often you use the VCR. Check the manual for the manufacturer's instructions.

If your last video failed to display on your screen or when it did show up it looked snowy, try playing a new blank tape. The blank tape cleans the heads, removing the dirt that blocks your view. Play the tape for an hour, remove it, then play one of your regular tapes.

If the picture is still snowy (or blank), try a tape-head cleaning videocassette. You can get one of two different types: a wet cleaning cassette that uses a special solution on the ribbon, and a dry cleaning cassette that uses gentle friction. Most experts recommend the wet type because the dry type is more likely to damage the VCR heads.

Mary's Handy Hints

To keep your VCR heads clean longer, check your rental tapes before playing them for signs of damage to the exterior of the tape. Fast-forward the tape past the first few minutes, where most damage occurs. In addition, fast-forward and rewind all your personal tapes every two years to prevent sticking.

Picture This: A Clean DVD Player

Dust is the enemy of all electronics, and that goes for DVD players, too; it builds up inside the machine, giving the DVD player eyestrain when it tries to read your discs.

Experts don't recommend cleaning discs for DVD players because the brush merely moves dust around inside the machine. Brushes can also scratch and damage the lens.

Some experts recommend opening the machine up and using a can of compressed air to blow out the dust, but this may void your warranty—and damage the DVD player. Your best bet is to follow the manufacturer's instructions that came with the player.

Dirt-Free Discs

Dirty CDs and DVDs can skip or stop playing altogether. Follow these steps for cleaning and repairing discs:

1. Hold the disc by the edges and the center hole.

2. Lightly dampen a clean antistatic cloth with disc cleaner.

3. Work the cloth from the inside hole to the outer edge following a straight line between the two edges. Circling the disc can damage it.

Keep your CDs and DVDs clean, and you'll be able to watch *Star Wars* and listen to Britney Spears until your family revolts.

Exposed! A Clean Camera

Photos capture all those moments you want to savor, from little Morgan's graduation from preschool to that embarrassing bachelor-party snafu when the cake collapsed on the dancer. So it makes good sense to take care of the camera that provides you with all these special memories. Follow these tips to keep your camera clicking away:

◆ Open the back of the camera (make sure there's no film in there!) and blow out the dust with a can of compressed air.

- Blow dust off the lens with compressed air, and then use a cloth made for camera lenses and a lens cleaner to wipe the lens. If your camera lens is plastic, use the paper tissues found in camera shops rather than the cleaning cloths. Most of the camera cloths are microfiber, which will scratch a plastic lens. Always place a drop of cleanser on the cloth and not directly onto the lens, because it may seep into the interior of the camera.

- Use a clean cloth barely dampened with water to clean the camera casing. Don't let water sneak its way into the camera's interior.

- Use a microfiber cloth to clean out the nooks and crannies in your camera's casing.

- Clean dirty battery contacts by rubbing them gently with a pencil eraser. Check manufacturer's guidelines before cleaning the battery contacts.

Voilà! Your camera is ready to immortalize many more fun, touching, and embarrassing moments in your life.

Mary's Handy Hints

Anything kept in the dark can grow moldy, including cameras. Airing your camera once a month for several days helps prevent lens mold, especially in areas of high humidity or heavy rainfall. In addition, place the silica packs found in vitamins and shoe boxes inside the camera case to help absorb moisture. Too late? Pour just a bit of hydrogen peroxide on the lens cloth and gently wipe the lens on both sides to remove mold.

Hold the Phone

The phone is something that we hold up against our face every day. When we have colds, we cough into the mouthpiece. We use our oily fingers on the keypad or dial. And yet, most of us never clean the thing.

Mary's Handy Hints

Erase your cordless troubles! If your cordless phone isn't charging, rub the metal contacts on the base unit with a clean pencil eraser to clean them. Then whisk away the eraser bits with a clean, soft brush such as an artist's paintbrush.

To clean the yucky stuff from your phone, wipe it down with a soft cloth and a bit of rubbing alcohol. Use a cotton swab dipped in rubbing alcohol to get into those little spaces where the cloth won't reach.

Polishing the Printer

Keeping your printer clean on the outside is easy: barely dampen a clean cloth with water or rubbing alcohol, and wipe down the case and the buttons. As for the printer's insides—there are so many different types of printers on the market, all with different cleaning needs, that it's best to consult the manufacturer's cleaning instructions.

Coming Clean with Your Computer

Your work is in there. Your recipes. Your photos. Your music files. Heck, your whole life is in your computer! Cleaning your computer will keep it functioning better—so you don't wind up looking at a blank screen and wondering how you'll ever live without all the data locked inside.

Here's how often you should clean your computer:

♦ If you don't smoke and have no pets, clean the computer every five months.

♦ If you don't smoke but do have pets, clean the computer every four months.

♦ If you smoke but have no pets, clean the computer every three months.

♦ If you smoke and have pets, clean the computer every two months.

Keyboard Cleanliness

Keyboards hold two kinds of dirt: First of all, dirt, dust, pet hair, and crumbs get inside the keyboard, which can eventually lead to a malfunction and have you typing things such as "hgf mwosu wyci fowenxx."

Second, germs build up on the keyboard, which can make *you* sick.

To eighty-six the internal dirt, hold your keyboard upside down over a wastebasket and shake it gently. Then hold it vertically over the wastebasket and use a can of compressed air between the keys to blow away the remaining dirt.

Then there are the germs. Turn off your computer and use a clean cloth barely dampened with a mixture of two parts vinegar, one part rubbing alcohol, and four parts water to give your keyboard keys a once over.

Mopping the Monitor

A smudged-up monitor can be hard on the eyes. For standard CRT screens, turn off the computer (to avoid getting a shock) and then lightly dampen a lint-free cloth with rubbing alcohol and wipe down the screen.

 Dirty Words

Never spray any liquid directly on a computer screen; it may drip under the edges and damage the delicate circuitry.

Don't use anything stronger than water on LCD screens; barely dampen a lint-free cloth with water and give the screen a gentle wiping. Do not use microfiber cloths on LCD screens. They can scratch the screen.

Freeing Your Fans from Dust

The fans in your computer keep the components cool. If the fans are encrusted with dust and goodness knows what else, they can work less efficiently or fail, causing your computer to overheat.

Never stack books, papers, or other objects against the side of a computer tower or monitor screen. It prevents the air from moving freely, causing the motors to overheat, which blows the circuits, which shuts down your computer, which causes you to spend more money getting a new computer.

If your tower is stored on the floor, place it on a solid hard surface such as a small sheet of plywood and not directly on the carpet. The dust from carpet fibers clogs the insides and the carpeting itself prevents the tower from cooling properly.

To clean the fans, first turn off your computer. Remove the case lid and locate the various fans. Using a can of compressed air, blow dust from the fans from the inside so that the dust is expelled out the back. Spray the air in short bursts. Blow away dust from the air vents in your case lid, too; if they're dusty, they can prevent the fans from expelling warm air.

An Open and Shut (and Clean) Case

To clean your computer's plastic case, simply wipe it down with a clean cloth barely dampened with water. For stubborn spots, use a bit of regular household detergent. Never use solvents on plastic.

Cleaning Quips

"My idea of super-woman is someone who scrubs her own floors."

—Bette Midler

Cleaning Your CD-ROM and Floppy Drives

A not-so-clean CD-ROM drive can cause read errors with CD discs. To clean your drive, run out to an electronics or office supply store and get a CD-ROM cleaner. Follow the instructions inside the box.

The same goes for dirty floppy drives: use a specialized cleaning kit from an electronics or office supply store.

Eek! A (Clean) Mouse!

Dirt on the ball or in the insides of your optical-mechanical computer mouse can make the mouse difficult to move and cause erratic mouse movement. And believe us, erratic mouse movement is something you don't want to see! Avoid the whole scenario by following these steps:

1. Remove the bottom cover of the mouse. Turn the mouse over and check to see which way the cover needs to be rotated. Place your fingers on the cover and move it in the direction of the arrows. Turn the mouse back over, and the bottom cover and the ball should fall right out.

2. You should see three rollers inside the mouse, most likely covered with greasy dirt and hair. Use a cotton swab to clean this grime off the rollers.

3. Clean the mouse ball with rubbing alcohol sprayed onto a clean cloth.

4. After you've de-grimed the inside of the mouse, replace the ball and the cover by reversing the directions in Step 1.

5. Clean the outside of the mouse by wiping with a cloth barely dampened with water or rubbing alcohol. This will keep it cleaner longer.

A clean mouse is a happy mouse—and it will keep you working away at your computer and surfing the Internet for a long time to come.

The Least You Need to Know

◆ Clean electronic devices work better and last longer than ones that are encrusted with filth.

◆ Always spray cleaner onto a cloth before wiping an electronic gadget—never spray the device directly.

◆ A can of compressed air is the electronics user's best friend.

◆ "Barely damp" are the keywords for electronics cleaning; whether you're using water, alcohol, or another cleaner, be sure to barely dampen your cleaning cloth.

Chapter 15

Speed Cleaning

In This Chapter

◆ Using the tools of the trade

◆ Knowing which formulas to follow

◆ Cleaning with super speed

◆ Hiring a professional

Your mother-in-law just called—she'll be popping over in 10 minutes. (Hey, at least she called this time.) The house looks like the first hour after a Christmas sale at J.C. Penney, and you haven't had a chance to vacuum up the masses of cat hair that cover every available surface. What to do?

You could blindfold your mother-in-law and convince her to play "blind man's bluff." You could lock the door and pretend you're not home. You could meet her on the front porch and take her out to a fancy brunch—hey, better to shell out some major moolah than to have her see your house in disarray. Or you could use the tips in this chapter to get your house in presentable order *tout de suite*. (That's French for "before the mother-in-law shows up.")

Tools of the Trade

If you're the type who tends to let things go and then speed clean at the last minute (or even if this only happens to you once in a while), you'll need special tools to accommodate your style. Try these:

- A big basket, such as a laundry basket. You can use this to quickly move items to their proper places in the house. If you're in a *really* big rush, you can toss in clutter and store the whole thing in a closet.

- A bucketless flat mop, such as the kind that has a container of cleaning solution attached. You can make the floors shine without having to fill and lug around a big bucket of water. Fill the container with water only so the chemicals that ordinarily come with the mops won't damage temperamental floor surfaces.

- A caddy for carrying cleaning supplies. Just like the professionals use! This lets you move from room to room without having to lug dozens of bottles and cloths.

- A spray bottle of water with 1 teaspoon of an all-natural liquid dishwashing soap like you find in a health food store. Regular dish soaps contain phosphorous, which smears on counter surfaces.

- A black ostrich-feather duster. This traps dust better than chicken feather dusters; 100 percent lambswool dusters are wonderful, too.

- Rubber gloves. Keep that manicure looking great!

- A lint roller. Get the kind that's made with sheets of sticky tape. You can use it to quickly roll pet hair off of upholstery, and also to get cobwebs off of textured ceilings and wood beams in a flash by putting two or three lint rollers onto a long handle with a paint roller attachment at the end.

Dirty Words

> Remember that ostrich feather dusters are black; colorful dusters may have feathers with plastic spines that can scratch your furniture.

- A cordless mini-vac. You can get these at discount stores for less than $20, and they're great for quickly picking up small messes such as scattered pet kibble or dirt on the floor.

These cleaning tools will help you zoom through the house in no time at all. Keep them organized and accessible, and you can grab them and get moving.

The Principles of Speed Cleaning

Here are some things you should keep in mind if you want to make short work of housework. These will help you keep things cleaner on a day-to-day basis so they'll need less scrubbing, and save you time when you *are* doing the housework.

Prevention, Prevention, Prevention

Ignoring dirt guarantees one thing: it's going to be a lot tougher to clean later on. A half inch of dust on the guest room furniture takes far longer to clean than a mere scattering. Leaving splattered food on a stovetop to bake on—well, we've all sweated over that chore.

Here we're going to get all scientific on you and introduce something called the "broken-window theory." Law enforcement officials found that if a house in a neighborhood had a broken window, it would suddenly attract vandals, graffiti artists, and other shady types. Soon, the whole neighborhood would be heading downhill. The theory is that criminals would see the broken window and suspect that no one cared about the condition of the house and no one was in charge.

The same thing happens in your house. It starts out clean. Then, one day, you leave a half-read newspaper on the family room couch. The next time you enter the family room, you're surprised to see a jacket draped over the easy chair, coffee cups on the coffee table, toys on the floor, and papers strewn over the side table. Now you have a huge mess to clean up! What happened?

According to the broken-window theory, that newspaper started the downward spiral. Other family members, seeing a tiny bit of disarray, felt free to add to the chaos.

The moral of the story: Try to clean as you go and keep things tidy, and others will show that same respect for your home. Squeegee the shower stall after showering and you won't lose the battle of the soap scum.

Rinse and then put bowls and pots in the dishwasher as you cook and you won't be faced with a towering stack of dishes when dinner is over. Clean that glop off the stovetop immediately and you won't waste time scrubbing after the glop becomes cooked on.

Mary's Handy Hints

Guests are coming and the air in your home is ... well, let's say less than fresh. Throw open a couple of windows and put a pot of water with a couple of cinnamon sticks on the stove to simmer. No cinnamon sticks? Use a bit of ground cinnamon or even other spices such as nutmeg or cloves. Instead of smelling like dog, last night's fish dinner, or whatever, your home will smell like you just baked a fresh pie. (Alternative solution: bake a fresh pie!)

Basket Case

Every day, walk through your home with a big basket, such as a laundry basket, and toss in anything that's out of place, such as the jacket on the family room couch, the toys in the kitchen, and the coffee cups in the living room. Put things back in their proper places, or have your family members come and take what's theirs from the basket.

A good habit to develop is never to leave a room without taking something with you to put away. Get the whole family involved! If a child is old enough to take out a toy, she is old enough to put it back (with Mom's or Dad's help at first, of course).

In our home, anything still in the basket after two weeks went to Goodwill. Amazingly, after the first trip to Goodwill that basket was empty by the next day!

Get a smaller basket to keep by the front door—you can hang it on the wall or keep it on a side table. This basket is where all papers entering the home go, from that business card you need to file to your kids' permission slips to the daily mail. Once a day, empty the basket (no, not into the trash, although it may be tempting).

Be Proud of Your Hang-Ups

Wall hooks are a busy housekeeper's best friend. Small hooks near the door hold keys, and bigger hooks in the entryway or garage hold coats and hats. Not only will you be able to find your stuff more easily if it's always in the same place, but you (and those last-minute guests) will be spared the sight of keys strewn on the coffee table and coats draped over every available surface.

Work It, Baby!

Give your product time to work. This is the single best timesaving tip we have to offer. If you have food stuck on the stovetop, spray it first and then continue cleaning. When you come back to the spot, the dirt is loosened and much easier to clean. Use this same principle in the bathroom.

Gather Your Tools

Keep all your cleaning tools organized and in one place so you can grab them and go. You can keep them in a basket or, like us, in a special caddy.

Divide and Conquer

To zip through cleaning, divide your home into four sections. The bedroom quadrant and hallway are section one. The kitchen, family room, and laundry areas are section two. Formal living rooms, dining rooms, and entryways are section three. Remote rooms such as dens and sunrooms are section four. Your sections, of course, will depend on the layout of your home.

Next, decide the order in which you'll clean your home. You generally want to start at the back of your home and work your way toward the center. If you have a two-story home, start on the second floor.

Is this yet another random rule that we made up when we were on a cleaning-related power trip? No—there is a good reason for it: you don't want to drag cleaning equipment through a freshly cleaned room.

Section cleaning involves cleaning every room in that section of your home completely before moving to the next section. It works best if you clean your entire home in one day. If you clean one section of your home one day and another section the next, it means pulling out all your equipment each time a section is cleaned. Your goal is to reduce unnecessary steps and time.

The Order of Things

Always clean from top to bottom; this will keep you from having to clean things twice. For example, if you dust and then knock down cobwebs from the ceiling, you'll have cobwebs all over your freshly dusted furniture.

Working from top to bottom will also get you to pay attention to high-up things you may have skipped over before, such as doorframes, picture frames, the ceiling, and your kids. (Boy, are they getting tall!)

Mary's Handy Hints

The great dusting/ vacuuming debate rages on, but Mary has the answer: dusting comes before vacuuming. When you dust, you knock dust from the furniture onto the floor, where the vacuum will then pick it up. If you vacuum first and then dust, you'll end up with dust all over your nice clean floors.

Always clean a room the same way and in the same direction each and every time you clean. It doesn't matter if you clean from left to right or right to left. Just clean the same way consistently. The secret to success in speed cleaning lies in repetition. As you become more and more familiar with the process, your speed increases.

Fast Formulas

If you want to learn math, you must memorize certain formulas. Okay, so this isn't a math book (thank goodness). But even in housecleaning, you need to master formulas if you're to become a super speed cleaner. Read on to find out how to clean every room in your house faster than you can say, "Hey, I just cleaned the house—now pick up those socks!"

Quick Kitchen Cleaning

Here's the formula you need to memorize to get your kitchen sparkling in record time. Remember, do it the same way every time so you don't have to think about it—you just go:

1. Place a coffee cup half full of water in the microwave. Cook on high for two minutes. The resulting steam loosens any baked on food for easy cleaning. While the water is heating, do the next step or two.

> **Mary's Handy Hints**
>
> Keep spare trash bags in the bottom of the trash can. That way when you empty the trash, you have another bag there and waiting!

2. Move appliances to one side, then spray all-purpose cleaner on the counter and any appliances in that immediate area, such as the dishwasher, refrigerator, or microwave. The reason for the mass spraying? Each time you put a bottle down and pick it up, you waste time.

3. While you have the all-purpose cleaner in hand, quickly look for food spots dried on the floor. Give those a squirt to speed floor cleaning.

4. As you work around the kitchen, wipe down the fronts of cabinets, paying special attention to door pulls.

5. Wipe down everything you sprayed.

6. Wipe out the microwave when you come to it.

7. Clean the sink following the instructions in Chapter 4.

8. Clean the floor following the instructions in Chapter 4.

Notice how in this formula, you're using the principles of working from top to bottom and leaving time for the products to work.

Breezing Through the Bathroom

You're sizzling now! Speed your way through the bathroom with this formula:

1. Spray the inside of the toilet with an all-purpose cleaner or an orange cleaner such as Bi-O-Kleen or Bio Ox. Let it sit while you do the following steps.

2. Spray the rim, toilet seat, countertop, and sink with your all-purpose cleaner.

3. Squirt the shower or tub walls with orange cleaner or other all-purpose cleaner.

4. Clean the toilet and toilet rim by sprinkling baking soda on your toilet bowl brush and giving the toilet a good scrub. (Make sure the brush doesn't have metal rings that can scratch the toilet.)

5. Spray only the part of the mirror that's dirty and wipe it down with a clean rag. That puts enough cleaner on the towel to clean the rest of the mirror.

6. Wipe down the counter, the sink, and the exterior of the toilet and the floor behind it.

7. Wipe down the shower walls, then spray the shower floor with all-purpose cleaner and clean it.

8. Finish by mopping the floor using the instructions in Chapter 9.

Once again, you're using the principles of working from top to bottom and allowing the products time to do their thing.

Fast-Forward Through the Family and Living Rooms

To rush through the family room and living room, you need to learn the very valuable skills of speed dusting and speed vacuuming. Get ready, set, go!

Mary's Handy Hints

People with arthritis or hand dexterity problems may find it helpful to place a rubber glove on their other hand to lift objects for a better grasp on the object.

1. Place an old, clean, cotton tube sock over your dusting hand and lightly dampen it with the cleaner you use to dust.

2. Spray a lint-free towel with the window cleaning solution—in a new 32-ounce spray bottle add ⅓ cup of (you guessed it) white

vinegar and ¼ cup rubbing alcohol, then fill with distilled water—and toss that over one shoulder to clean any glass in tables or cabinets.

3. Lift objects with one hand, then dust with the other.

4. Begin dusting from either the right or the left and work your way around the room, dusting window sills and wall hangings as you come to them. As you dust furniture, move it so you can later vacuum behind it.

5. For homes with pets, tuck a clean pair of rubber gloves into your back pocket. When you come to couches or chairs with pet hair, use the gloves and work your hands in a circular motion moving over the furniture. You can also use a "dry" sponge. These are specially treated sponges that pick up not only dog or cat hair but also surface dust and dirt. Toss the rolled up lint onto the floor for the vacuum to pick up.

6. Vacuum around the room in the same order you dusted. Vacuum behind furniture first, finishing with the center. Back your way out of the room.

> **Mary's Handy Hints**
>
> Add a 15- to 25-foot extension cord to your vacuum cleaner to save time moving the cord from room to room.

Ah, bliss. The living areas are now livable again, and it hardly took any time at all. You deserve a lemonade!

Bustling Through the Bedroom

It's easy to forget bedrooms—just close the door and be done with it, says the little devil perched on your shoulder. But cleaning the bedroom is as easy as pie with these steps:

1. Tidy the room. Empty the trash can and pick up clothes and other items that aren't where they belong. Make the bed.

2. Dust from top to bottom. Spot clean with a barely damp cloth as you move around the room.

3. Vacuum the carpet or use a floor duster on the floor.

That's it! It's so much nicer to retire to a clean and tidy bedroom at night than to something that resembles the set of a disaster movie.

Emergency! When You Only Have an Hour

Okay, you're so rushed for time that even our speed cleaning formulas aren't speedy enough for you. Guests are coming in an hour, and you really don't have time to clean the tub or shine chrome handles or clean the microwave. You just want the place to look presentable!

Not to worry—you have enough time to make your house clean enough for a visit from even the fussiest of guests. After all, it took Einstein only an hour to come up with the theory of relativity. (Okay, so we made that up. But doesn't it make cleaning the house in an hour seem like a snap?)

1. Get it together. Get out your cleaning caddy or basket of cleaning products. Barely dampen a soft cloth and throw it over one shoulder, and throw a dry cloth over the other shoulder. Attach a large garbage bag to your belt or tote so you can empty trash cans as you come to them.

2. Hide it. Toss everything that's not where it belongs (toys, plates, old newspapers) into the laundry basket to put away later. Put the basket in a closet.

3. Hit the kitchen. In the kitchen, put dirty dishes in the dishwasher and wipe down the counters with all-purpose cleaner (unless they're marble, granite, or tile, in which case you should follow the directions in Chapter 4). Wipe any fingerprints from appliances and around light switches and cabinet pulls. A sparkling sink makes any kitchen look cleaner, so clean yours using instructions in Chapter 4. If you have a stainless-steel sink, shine it with a dab of baby oil on a cloth. Quickly mop the floor with plain water.

4. Swipe the bathroom. Spray down the sink and toilet, then wipe down. Clean the toilet bowl using the instructions earlier in this chapter. Close the shower curtain so you don't have to bother cleaning out the tub or shower stall (and hope no one peeks back there).

5. Blast through the living room (and family room). Use the ostrich-feather duster to dust the TV, knickknacks, lampshades, and picture frames. Wipe wood furniture with a barely damp cloth and dry. Use a lint roller, rubber glove, or the upholstery attachment on your vacuum to clean the couch and loveseat. Vacuum the carpet or floor. (Don't bother to move the furniture.)

6. Run through the rest of the house. Close the doors to the bedrooms. Finally, dim the lights!

If you've kept up with your regular cleaning, this super speed cleaning should be a cinch. And even if you haven't, you can use the principles here to get your home in presentable shape until you can clean it again. Now wipe the sweat from your brow, answer the doorbell, and enjoy your guests!

Going Pro: Hiring a Professional

 **Cleaning Quips**

"My second favorite household chore is ironing. My first being hitting my head on the top bunk bed until I faint."

—Erma Bombeck

If you find yourself always trying to beat the clock when it comes to cleaning your home—and never seeming to get ahead—it might be time to hire a professional housecleaner.

Choosing a Cleaning Service

Grab a clipboard, paper, and pen and start answering the following questions. This initial exercise will guide you in your selection of a company as well as the kind of service that best suits your home and lifestyle:

- What will your budget allow? Cleaning fees can run $40 to $150 per visit. If your budget is tight, plan on an every-other-week cleaning.

◆ Do you have any problems that need to be addressed? Walk through your home and jot down notes of any problem areas. If the dog or cat is prone to accidents or toilet leaks cause water stains, the company must know. Water that is either hard or contains iron can also be problematic. The pros' choice of products as well as their ability to thoroughly clean your home depends on these details.

◆ What do you want cleaned? Other than the general cleaning such as dusting, mopping, vacuuming, kitchen, and bathrooms, what other areas do you want cleaned? Do you have a laundry room or mini-blinds? What about ceiling fans? Do you want the sheets on your bed changed? Also, decide what you *don't* want cleaned with every visit.

Some cleaning people will do the laundry, but we don't recommend this. Too many people just don't know how to care for clothes, and there's a chance that your favorite sweater will end up becoming your 5-year-old daughter's favorite sweater when it shrinks down to child size.

Seeking a Specialist

You now know what you're looking for—so how do you find this mythical cleaning service that can erase your toilet rings, work according to your schedule, fit into your budget, and get your kids into Harvard on full scholarship? Here are some ways:

◆ A personal reference from a friend. This is the best way to find a company or an independent cleaning person. Friends have generally hired and possibly fired a few companies and can help with your selection.

◆ Janitorial supply companies. Call several until you hear the same name (companies or individuals) repeated a couple of times.

◆ The newspaper or Yellow Pages. Look for ads that reflect the type of service that suits both you and your home.

Making the Call

Revert to the days of your childhood when your inquisitive mind asked all kinds of questions, from why the sky is blue to where babies come from. The questions you ask and subsequent answers (or lack of them) will direct you to the right cleaning person or cleaning company.

Here are a few examples of questions to ask. Base your questions on the information you gathered about your individual needs.

◆ Do they clean once a week or will they come every other week? If your budget or life-style allow only for twice-monthly visits, this question is important.

◆ Do they clean for special occasions such as a wedding? Special occasions will come up and you may need a helping hand with the cleaning or other prep work.

> **Dishing the Dirt**
>
> A company or individual cleaner will not be able to give you a firm bid over the phone. The final cost for the cleaning depends on the size of your home, number of pets, number of children, and the amount of furnishings, among other things.

◆ Are they bonded and insured? *Insured* means they are covered in case of damage to your property. *Bonded* protects you should anything in your home turn up missing.

◆ Do they charge by the job or by the hour? If they charge by the job, ask how long they typically spend in a home your size. One person cannot thoroughly clean a 2,400-square-foot home in 2 hours—unless their idea of "thoroughly cleaning" is to race through your house swiping everything with a wet rag.

◆ What do they cover during each visit? Do they include "extras" such as dusting cobwebs and cleaning smudged windows?

◆ Do they bring their own equipment? This is preferable, but let them know you want to approve the cleaners they use and that they should bring a list with them to the initial meeting.

◆ If it's a cleaning company you're questioning, does the owner do the cleaning or do they hire employees? If they hire employees, does the owner or a trainer come with the employee for the first two or three cleanings? This is preferable. It's important to have a fully trained person helping the employee clean difficult areas such as hard-water rings in toilets and soap residue buildup in showers.

◆ If they send employees to clean your home, will you be assigned a permanent cleaning person? It takes several cleanings to become familiar with the layout of a home. When a cleaning professional becomes familiar with the home, cleaning speed increases, making it possible to schedule in extra jobs such as ceiling fan blades. You don't want a new person cleaning your home every visit.

Listen closely to their answers. Did they take time to fully answer your questions or pressure you for a home visit? If you felt like the person was putting the squeeze on you, call another company.

After you've hired a professional, you'll never be racing against the clock to clean your house again!

The Least You Need to Know

◆ Having the right tools will let you clean the house in no time at all.

◆ Always work from top to bottom, and in the same direction around each room.

◆ Cleaning will be easier if you prevent messes from happening in the first place.

◆ Remember that old saying, "A place for everything, and everything in its place"? It's oh, so true. Make use of baskets and hooks to keep things where they belong.

◆ These tips not strong enough for you? Consider hiring a professional so your home always stays clean.

Your Complete Stain-Removal Guide

So you spilled something on something else. No worries! This appendix tells you how to get just about any substance off of just about any surface.

General Guidelines

Before you start blotting and wiping and spraying away, let's get a few things straight:

- ◆ Always test an inconspicuous spot on whatever surface before you go whole hog with the stain removal.

- ◆ Give your product time to work. Apply the cleaner and allow it to set undisturbed for at least 15 minutes.

- ◆ If we suggest using a concentrated orange cleaner, try to find one without petroleum distillates, which may be listed on the label as mineral spirits, aliphatic hydrocarbon, or hydrocarbon.

- ◆ Clean a spill immediately. The longer it sets, the harder it is to remove the stain.

- Use a clean white rag to remove a stain, because the color from a rag can transfer onto the surface you're cleaning.

- Frequently move the cloth so that a clean surface is showing to keep the stain from spreading.

- On fabrics, begin spraying the cleaner from the outer edges of the stain, and work your way toward the center of the stain. This keeps the stain from spreading.

- Keep a bottle of enzyme cleaner on hand for cleaning urine, vomit, and all organic stains and spills. By the time you run out to the store to buy a bottle, the stain can set!

These tips can save you a lot of work—giving you more time to sip lemonade and relax on your porch swing.

Carpet Stain-Removal Guidelines

Whenever we're talking about removing a stain from carpet, follow these cleaning guidelines with the suggested stain-removal product:

- Always blot; never rub. Rubbing breaks down the fibers and weakens the material.

- Blot correctly. To blot, punch your index knuckle into a rag dampened with ¼ cup white vinegar per quart of water. Work your knuckle forward and backward, and then left to right, across the stain in the carpet; then twist your wrist in a clockwise direction. Carpet fibers are twisted clockwise. This motion removes stains from between the fibers without causing the carpet to fuzz.

- Clean it big. When any kind of liquid has spilled into carpet, it hits the padding and spreads. What looks like a baseball-size stain on top of the carpet is actually the size of a beach ball on the padding. You must clean an area of carpet at least twice as large as the surface stain when treating any liquid stain that is more than 2 or 3 ounces of liquid.

- Work carefully with peroxide. When you remove a stain from carpeting using hydrogen peroxide, do not allow it to remain on the carpet longer than 20 to 30 minutes. Many carpets are made partly from Olefin, and peroxide can leave a greenish stain on these carpets.

♦ Rinse any cleaner away with ¼ cup white vinegar per quart of water, and then again with plain water, taking care not to over-saturate the carpet.

Now, on to the good stuff!

Stain-Removal Secrets

Beer on the upholstery? Soot on the walls? Mascara on the carpet? (Hey, it happens.) Here's what you need to know to remove common stains from various surfaces. Remember to refer to the "General Guidelines" and "Carpet Stain-Removal Guidelines" for more information.

Ballpoint Ink

Carpet: Use a cotton swab to apply rubbing alcohol to help prevent the stain from spreading. Wait 15 minutes and blot. Repeat if needed, giving the alcohol a bit longer to dissolve the ink. Rinse.

Fabric furniture and mattresses: Try a squirt of white foaming shaving cream. Spray on just enough shaving cream to cover the spot and wait 30 minutes. Wipe off the excess and rinse.

Laminated/wood floor and wood furniture: Apply just a small amount of rubbing alcohol to the spot. After five minutes, wipe to remove. Reapply if needed. If rubbing alcohol does not remove the ink, then try white (i.e., nongel) foaming shaving cream. As a last resort, lightly sand the floor using a 0000 steel-wool pad. Call the flooring manufacturer for their recommendations for a sealer to restore the finish. For furniture, condition the piece with a high-quality furniture wax.

Dishing the Dirt

You may read recommendations to use hairspray for ink removal. Hairspray contains alcohol, which is the ingredient that removes the ink. The other chemicals in hair spray could damage a fabric. Take caution should you decide to use hairspray on a stain.

Leather/vinyl: You can remove ink from leather and vinyl only with a product specifically made for those surfaces. Most leather cleaners will not remove ink, so talk to the manufacturer before purchasing the product.

Linoleum floors: Rub with a bit of toothpaste.

Walls: Rub with a bit of toothpaste or use a white Mr. Clean pad.

Beer and Alcohol

Carpet: Blot the stain and apply enzyme cleaner. Wait an hour or longer, giving the enzymes plenty of time to "eat" the bacteria. Rinse.

Fabric furniture: Read and follow the manufacturer's cleaning guide. Remove the cushion if possible and immediately rinse in a solution of 1 gallon of cool water plus ½ cup of white vinegar. Soak the foam in the tub, following the same dilution of vinegar to water. Air dry both sections. If the cushion is not removable, soak the whole cushion as described if the fabric is machine washable.

Laminated/wood floor: Wipe immediately and apply a small amount of an enzyme cleaner. Wait no longer than five minutes, and then rinse with ¼ cup of white vinegar per quart of water. Dry immediately. Contact the manufacturer for the proper method to restore the wood should it turn dark, mold, or continue to smell. If the wood warps, the floor will need to be sanded and refinished. You cannot sand and refinish laminated floors.

Leather/vinyl: Wipe immediately with a mild detergent such as Woolite. Wait until the spot has dried for 24 hours to make sure the stain has been removed. (It may be necessary to clean it a second time.) Once the leather is dry, apply a high-quality leather and vinyl conditioner to prevent cracking and drying.

Linoleum: Remove the excess moisture. Clean the floor with ¼ teaspoon of mild liquid dishwashing soap per quart of water. Rinse with ¼ cup white vinegar to ½ gallon of water, and then again with plain water. Dry immediately.

Mattresses: Professionally clean to remove both the odor and stain.

Tile, marble, granite floors: Spray with an enzyme cleaner, wait five minutes, rinse with hot water only, and immediately dry. Do not use vinegar or any cleaners because they will pit and damage the flooring.

Walls: Clean with nonalkali liquid dishwashing soap using minimal water. Rinse with straight vinegar. You may need to seal and repaint the surface to remove the stains.

Wood furniture: Stains of this nature will darken and possibly warp the wood. Clean with ¼ cup white vinegar per quart of water. Dry, then wait several days to see if the wood will be darkened. It may be necessary to sand and refinish the furniture. If the wood has not darkened, apply a high-quality wood conditioner.

Berry Stains

Carpet, upholstery, and mattresses: Pour straight 3 percent hydrogen peroxide on the stain and let it set for 20 minutes. Rinse. Repeat if needed after 24 hours. Borax also does a good job removing berry stains; use 1 teaspoon per quart of water and follow the directions described here.

Laminated/wood floor: Wood floors need to be sanded and refinished; call a professional. Laminated floors can be safely cleaned with hydrogen peroxide. Most laminated floors do not stain easily.

Leather/vinyl: Berry stains are nearly impossible to remove from leather and vinyl. Saturate a paper towel with straight hydrogen peroxide and lay it on the stain, weighing the paper towel down with a cooking pan. Wait one to two hours, keeping the towel damp. Rinse with plain water and dry. Follow with a leather/vinyl conditioner. Whitening toothpaste will sometimes remove a berry stain; rub on a bit, rinse, and blot.

Tile, marble, granite floors: The StainEraser is the only item that will remove berry stains from grout.

Walls: Rub gently with a Mr. Clean white cleaning pad.

Wood furniture: Use 3 percent hydrogen peroxide, but go easy because it can bleach the wood. Apply, wait 5 to 10 minutes, and blot with ¼ cup white vinegar per quart of water. If the wood bleaches, use the meat of a walnut or pecan to restore the color. Treat with wood conditioner.

Blood

Carpet and upholstery: Immediately blot with a 50/50 solution of cool water and 3 percent hydrogen peroxide. Repeat until the blood is gone. Rinse. Enzyme cleaners are also excellent for removing blood stains.

Wood/laminated floors and wood furniture: Blood is difficult to remove from wood and it will usually darken the wood, which can be lightened some with hydrogen peroxide. Use great care when bleaching wood. Wipe immediately, and then blot with ¼ cup white vinegar to one quart cool water.

Leather/vinyl: Clean with cold water or 3 percent hydrogen peroxide.

Mattresses: Spray with an enzyme cleaner or straight 3 percent hydrogen peroxide. Rinse.

Tile, marble, granite floors: For white grout, spray with 3 percent peroxide until the blood is gone. For colored grout, rinse with cold water, wait until the grout has dried, and then use The StainEraser to remove the rest.

Walls: Rub gently with a Mr. Clean white cleaning pad.

> **Dishing the Dirt**
>
> Always wear rubber gloves when cleaning another person's blood, even if it's a close friend or family member. Hepatitis C and other diseases are spread by blood contact; the person may not know he or she is a carrier because it can take years to discover.

Chocolate

Carpet: Immediately dab on liquid dishwashing soap that contains no alkalis and wait 30 to 60 minutes. Rinse and repeat if needed. Use a 50/50 solution of hydrogen peroxide to water if any stain remains.

Fabric furniture: See the "Carpet" section or use white foaming shaving cream. Rinse.

Grout in stone flooring: Use white foaming shaving cream. Spray on, wait at least 15 minutes, and wipe up.

Walls: Dab on a nonalkali liquid dishwashing detergent. Rinse using as little moisture as possible.

Wood furniture: See the "Grease and Oil" section.

Coffee or Cola

Carpet: For large spills, follow the advice in the "Carpet Stain-Removal Guidelines" section (beginning of the appendix). For small spills, a light spritz of a 50/50 solution of hydrogen peroxide to water usually removes the stain. Rinse with plain water. Or dilute 1 tablespoon borax per quart of water, blot, and rinse.

Fabric furniture and mattresses: Spray on white foaming shaving cream, wait 15 to 20 minutes, and rinse.

Laminated/wood floor and wood furniture: Wipe immediately. If water spots remain from larger spills, use a good wood cleaner and conditioner made to remove water spots from furniture.

Tile, marble, granite floors: Peroxide or The StainEraser for white grout; The StainEraser for any colored grout.

Walls: Blot on 3 percent hydrogen peroxide. Repeat every 30 minutes until the stain is gone.

Cooking Oil (Including Bacon, Butter, Lard, and Vegetable Oil)

See the "Grease and Oil" section or try an enzyme cleaner on all surfaces. Follow bottle directions when using an enzyme cleaner, and remember to give the enzymes plenty of time to do their job.

Crayon

Carpet and upholstery: Freeze the crayon with an ice cube tucked inside a zip-lock bag. Scrape off what you can with a blunt knife. A solvent is needed to remove most crayon marks; try a concentrated orange cleaner first. Use the cleaner concentrated, rubbing a bit into the carpet, twisting clockwise with your index finger and thumb. Wait 30 to 60 minutes, then blot. Rinse. It will take several rinses to remove a concentrated cleaner.

A product called DeSolvIt also does a good job removing crayon. With either product, be careful not to work the cleaner down to the backing. Either will dissolve the adhesive holding the fibers to the pad.

Laminated/wood floor: Freeze the crayon with an ice cube tucked inside a zip-lock bag. Scrape off what you can with a plastic scraper, being careful not to scratch the floor. Turn on the hair dryer to the highest heat. Begin heating the crayon, dabbing with a cloth as it melts. Be careful not to overheat the flooring or push the crayon into the seams. Never use an iron on any kind of flooring, carpet, or hard surface.

Leather/vinyl: Use a mild solvent such as DeSolvIt. Wipe on, wait 20 to 30 minutes, and then blot to remove. Follow with a mild detergent such as Woolite, and rinse with plain water only. Apply a leather and vinyl conditioner.

Linoleum: Freeze with ice, chipping off what you can with a blunt knife. Finish with DeSolvIt or a concentrated orange cleaner.

Tile, marble, granite floors: Scrape off marble and granite surfaces with a plastic scraper. Use the heat from a hair dryer to remove anything that's left. For tile floors, freeze with an ice cube inside a zip-lock bag. Scrape away what you can with a plastic scraper. Try using a clean, soft cloth dipped in boiling water to melt the rest. Solvents of any kind will ruin a tile floor.

Walls: Never use a solvent on a wall, because it will leave a permanent stain and prevent paint from sticking to the wall. Dip a cloth in boiling hot water with a bit of liquid dishwashing soap. Blot the spot only. Any rubbing will remove the paint, especially flat paint. It is better to apply a primer and paint over the spot rather than chance staining the wall with a solvent.

Wood furniture: This depends on the type of finish. For hard, slick finishes, wipe off what you can with a clean cloth, and then set your hair dryer to hot and melt the crayon to remove the rest. It is best to call an expert refinisher for advice on antique furniture, because what is safe for some antiques will ruin others. For tung oil finishes, freeze the crayon with ice and use a plastic scraper to scrape off what you can. Then place a clean, white, soft cloth on top of the stain. Set your iron to medium low heat and quickly iron over the remainder. Do not hold the iron on the spot—move quickly to prevent any damage to the wood.

Dirt

Carpet, mattresses, and upholstery: Dampen a clean white cloth with warm water, and then pour a drop of liquid dish washing detergent on the cloth. Gently blot the spot and rinse.

Laminated/wood floor and wood furniture: Clean with ¼ cup white vinegar to 1 quart of water.

Walls: Wipe the dirt off with an all-purpose cleaner.

> ### Dishing the Dirt
>
> If your dirt begins as mud, wait until the mud has dried, and then brush or vacuum away what you can before using a cleaner.

Dye

Carpet and upholstery: *Red dye 40 as found in dog food, cat food, popsicles, Kool-Aid, and punch:* Spray with 3 percent hydrogen peroxide. Allow it to set for no longer than 20 to 30 minutes, and then blot and rinse. *Hair dye:* Call a carpet-cleaning company, because anything you do will only spread the stain.

Grout: If The StainEraser doesn't take it out, nothing will.

> ### Dishing the Dirt
>
> Dye will not come out of leather, vinyl, linoleum, laminated or wood floors, mattresses, walls, or wood furniture.

Feces

Carpet and upholstery: Feces must be removed with an enzyme product. Spray on enough product to saturate to the padding. Follow the bottle directions. Blot to remove. Rinse with plain water and dry. Repeat if needed.

Laminated/wood floor: Use minimal amounts of enzyme cleaner, because wood and laminated flooring will not tolerate much moisture. Wipe on, wait five minutes, and then rinse with ¼ cup white vinegar per quart of water. Dry immediately.

Leather/vinyl: Use an enzyme product following the instructions on the label.

Linoleum: Use an enzyme product following the instructions on the label.

Mattresses: If the "accident" was caused by diarrhea, it's best to have the mattress professionally cleaned as it's difficult to remove all the stain and odor.

Tile, marble, granite floors: Use an enzyme product following the instructions on the label.

Food

See the "Individual Stains" section.

Glue and Adhesive

Carpet and mattresses: Freeze the glue with an ice cube placed in a zip-lock bag. Scrape off what you can with a plastic scraper, and then use an undiluted concentrated orange cleaner or DeSolvIt. Dab a bit on your index finger and twist onto the spot clockwise using your index finger and thumb. Wait 30 to 60 minutes, and then blot and rinse. If you're using DeSolvIt, rinse with a liquid dishwashing soap before rinsing with vinegar and water. Repeat if needed. Work carefully so as not to work the cleaner into the padding; either product will dissolve the adhesive holding the fiber to the backing.

Fabric furniture: Freeze as described for glue and adhesives in carpet and mattresses and scrape off what you can with a plastic scraper. Blot on an undiluted concentrated orange cleaner or DeSolvIt using a cotton swab to prevent spreading the stain. Wait 20 to 30 minutes, gently blot, and rinse following the guidelines for carpet and mattresses.

Laminated/wood floor, wood furniture, tile, marble, granite: Concentrated oil cleaners and DeSolvIt can ruin the sealant on wood or laminated floor. First freeze as you would for carpet, and then scrape off what you can with a plastic scraper. Then apply a bit of smooth peanut butter, wait five minutes, and gently blot. Sometimes the oil from peanut butter will dissolve any remaining glue. If the peanut butter does not work, it is best to contact the floor manufacturer for their recommendations.

Leather/vinyl: Good luck. This one is rough as the glue works down into either fabric and is quite tough to remove. Freeze like you would for carpet then scrape away all that is possible. Apply a concentrated orange cleaner (never DeSolvIt) to remove it and wait 30 minutes. Gently blot with a damp cloth. Repeat if needed. Rinse with warm water, dry immediately, and apply a leather/vinyl conditioner.

Linoleum: Freeze with an ice cube in a zip-lock bag and scrape off what you can with a plastic scraper. Remove any excess with either an undiluted concentrated orange cleaner or DeSolvIt.

Walls: Freeze as you would for carpet. Apply a primer and paint over the spot, because removing glue or adhesive from a wall will remove the paint.

Grease (Auto) and Motor Oil

Carpet: First try applying rubbing alcohol to the spot with a cotton swab. Wait 15 to 20 minutes and blot. Repeat if the stain is coming out, otherwise dab an undiluted concentrated orange cleaner on your finger and work into the spot by twisting the fibers clockwise between your finger and thumb. Use caution not to work the orange cleaner near the base of the carpet, because it will dissolve the adhesive holding the fibers to the padding. Now wait at least 30 to 60 minutes. Blot. Repeat if needed, and then rinse. You will need to rinse several times to remove all the concentrated cleaner.

Fabric furniture: Dab on an undiluted concentrated orange cleaner with a cotton swab. Wait 20 to 30 minutes and blot gently. Repeat if needed. White foaming shaving cream may also be used. Use as you would concentrated orange cleaner.

Laminated/wood floor and wood furniture: Remove what you can with a dry, soft, clean 100 percent cotton cloth—not terry. Apply just a small amount of rubbing alcohol. Wait five minutes and rinse with ¼ cup white vinegar per quart of water and dry immediately. Repeat if needed—just do not allow the alcohol to remain on the wood for longer than five minutes at a time. Give the wood time to completely dry before reapplying the alcohol.

Leather/vinyl: White foaming shaving cream is your best bet for leather and vinyl. It contains two or three kinds of alcohol and has a better chance of removing grease or oil from leather than straight alcohol alone. Plus it does not immediately run off the surface so it has time to dissolve the oil. Spray on the spot and wait 15 to 20 minutes. Gently rub with a soft cloth and rinse with plain water. Always follow with a good-quality leather cleaner and conditioner.

Linoleum: Rubbing alcohol should remove the grease and oil. Put plenty on the spot, then let it set for 10 to 15 minutes. Blot with a soft cloth. If the alcohol alone does not work, use white foaming shaving cream.

Mattresses: Use white foaming shaving cream; apply, let it set for 15 minutes, and blot.

Tile, marble, granite floors: Remove what you can with a clean, soft cloth. Rubbing alcohol soaks right through tile floors if poured directly on the tile. Try white foaming shaving cream first, allowing it to set between 5 and 10 minutes. Reapply if needed. If that doesn't work, try mixing a paste of rubbing alcohol and baking soda. Apply, wait 5 to 10 minutes, and then gently remove. For marble and granite, use straight rubbing alcohol (no baking soda).

Walls: Mix a paste of rubbing alcohol and cornstarch. Plaster on the spot and let that set for 45 to 60 minutes. Apply a paint primer, and then touch up the spot with leftover paint.

Wood furniture: Rubbing alcohol will remove grease and oil from sealed furniture. Apply, wait no longer than five minutes, and remove with a soft cloth. Repeat if needed. For tung oil finishes, pour on enough cornstarch to thoroughly cover the stain, gently pressing it into the wood. Wait 30 to 60 minutes and vacuum off the cornstarch. Keep applying until no more oil is absorbed. Then dab on just a bit of rubbing alcohol with a cotton swab and follow the directions above. Apply furniture wax to all furniture surfaces to restore the wood's luster.

Gum

General rule for removing gum from any surface: freeze the gum with a cube of ice in a zip-lock bag. Use a plastic scraper to chip away all you can. Repeat until most of the gum has been removed, and then follow the directions for your surface.

Carpet: Any remaining gum can be removed by applying DeSolvIt or an undiluted concentrated orange cleaner, letting it set for 15 minutes, and rinsing. If using DeSolvIt, rinse with liquid dishwashing detergent to remove the cleaner and then follow up with the vinegar and water.

Fabric furniture and mattresses: Use undiluted concentrated orange cleaner (not DeSolvIt) to remove anything that remains after freezing. Apply with a cotton swab, wait 15 to 30 minutes, and gently blot. You may need to rinse several times.

Laminated/wood floor, wood furniture, and linoleum: If all the gum has not been removed, apply real mayonnaise to soften the remaining gum. Rinse with ¼ cup white vinegar per quart of water. On wood, follow with a high-quality wax for wood furniture.

Leather/vinyl: Apply an undiluted concentrated orange cleaner to remove any residue. Dab on with a cotton swab, wait five minutes, and then rinse several times with ¼ cup white vinegar per quart of water. Apply a leather/vinyl conditioner.

Tile, marble, granite floors: Remove any remaining gum with real mayonnaise, and then clean with a liquid dishwashing soap. Rinse with hot water only, no vinegar. Do not use orange cleaner or solvents on marble, granite, or tile floors.

Walls: The wall will need to be painted after chipping away the gum, because it will take the paint off. Use a primer first, and then paint the spot.

Hair Dye

See the "Dye" section.

Hand Lotion

Carpet and upholstery: Apply white foaming shaving cream and let it set 15 to 20 minutes, and then rinse.

Laminated/wood floor and wood furniture: First pour cornstarch onto the stain, gently working it into the wood, and then wait 30 minutes. Vacuum the cornstarch away and repeat the process until the cornstarch no longer absorbs oil. Vacuum any remaining cornstarch. Remove any remaining lotion with rubbing alcohol. Do not leave the alcohol on longer than 5 to 10 minutes. Let the wood dry thoroughly and reapply if needed. Use a wax to restore the luster in wood furniture.

Leather/vinyl: Absorb what you can with cornstarch, and then wipe with rubbing alcohol. If any lotion remains, apply a bit of white foaming shaving cream, let it set for five minutes, and rinse with ¼ cup white vinegar per quart of water.

Linoleum: Spray with rubbing alcohol and wipe up.

Mattresses: Apply rubbing alcohol, wait five minutes, and rinse.

Tile, marble, granite floors: Cornstarch should remove most of the lotion from tile floors. Finish with rubbing alcohol and rinse with hot water only. For marble and granite, use rubbing alcohol only.

Walls: Mix a paste of cornstarch and water. Plaster the mixture on the spot, wait 30 minutes, and vacuum off the cornstarch. Finish with rubbing alcohol. The lotion will leave a stain, so use a primer and then paint.

Iodine and Metholide

Carpet, upholstery, and mattresses: Rinse immediately with cool water, working from the outer area inward toward the center. Keep blotting, turning the towel often. If any iodine or metholide remains, try rubbing alcohol or a 50/50 solution of hydrogen peroxide to water, and then rinse.

Laminated/wood floor and wood furniture: Use cool water only. If the stain doesn't come out, it's seeped into the wood fibers. You may be able to sand and refinish the wood, but it's best to contact a professional.

Leather/vinyl: Blot with cool water. If this doesn't work, try rubbing alcohol. White foaming shaving cream may budge the stubborn areas;

spray it on and let it set for 15 minutes, and then rinse thoroughly with cool water.

Linoleum: Use cool water. If the iodine or metholide seeps into the sublayers, the stain will be permanently set.

Tile, marble, granite floors: Blot with cool water. If this doesn't work, try rubbing alcohol.

Walls: Blot with cool water. If this doesn't work, try rubbing alcohol. Prime and repaint if needed.

Juice

See the "Kool-Aid, Popsicles, Punch, and Grape Juice" section.

Kool-Aid, Popsicles, Punch, and Grape Juice

These stains are all caused by red dye 40 except for grape juice, but they're treated the same way. Immediately sponge 3 percent peroxide onto the spot and let it set for 15 to 20 minutes. Rinse. This treatment may also work for wood, but it can take the color out. If this is the case, you can restain it, or try rubbing it with the meat of a walnut or pecan to bring back the color.

Lipstick

Carpet: Dab an undiluted concentrated orange cleaner on your finger and work into the spot by twisting the fibers clockwise between your finger and thumb. Use caution not to work the orange cleaner near the base of the carpet, because it will dissolve the adhesive holding the fibers to the padding. Now wait at least 30 to 60 minutes. Blot. Repeat if needed, then rinse. You will need to rinse several times to remove all the concentrated cleaner.

Fabric furniture and mattresses: Dab on an undiluted concentrated orange cleaner with a cotton swab. Wait 20 to 30 minutes and blot gently. Repeat if needed. White foaming shaving cream may also be used. Use as you would concentrated orange cleaner.

Leather/vinyl: Dab on an undiluted concentrated orange cleaner with a cotton swab, wait five minutes, and then rinse several times with ¼ cup white vinegar per quart of water. Follow with a leather/vinyl conditioner.

Linoleum: Rub the stain with a cloth dampened in detergent and warm water. If this doesn't work, rub with steel wool dipped in water and detergent. If the floor is hard surfaced, "no-wax," or embossed vinyl asbestos, use a plastic scouring pad instead of steel wool. After removing a stain, rinse the area thoroughly, dry completely, and, if floor finish has been removed in that area, recoat with appropriate finish or wax.

Magic Marker

Carpet, fabric furniture, and mattresses: Sponge on a small amount of dry-cleaning solvent, and then blot. Mix one teaspoon of a mild non-alkaline nonbleaching detergent with a cup of lukewarm water. Sponge it on, and then blot. Dab the spot with rubbing alcohol and blot. Finally, rinse.

Laminated/wood floor and wood furniture: When the label reads *permanent*, that means *permanent*. If the mark is deep into the wood, it may be necessary to lightly sand the wood with very fine sandpaper. Then use a wood conditioner to restore the wood.

Tile: Spray with Motsenbocker's Lift Off #3. Spray the stain thoroughly, wait at least 60 seconds, and then wipe with a clean towel. Repeat if necessary.

Leather/vinyl: Felt-tip markers may respond to treatment with mineral spirits. Blot the stain with a clean white cloth dampened with mineral spirits. Rinse with a damp cloth and a bit of liquid dishwashing soap, and then with plain water. Allow the area to dry and immediately treat with a good leather/vinyl cleaner and conditioner. Mineral spirits will dry and crack leather and vinyl, so use caution and use minimal amounts when applying it.

Walls: Sorry! You'll have to apply a primer and repaint the spot.

Mascara and Makeup

Carpet and fabric furniture: Sponge with a small amount of dry-cleaning solvent, and then blot. Then mix 1 teaspoon of a neutral detergent containing no alkalis or bleaches with a cup of lukewarm water and blot it on. Finally, sponge with clean water and blot.

Corian or marble bathroom counters: If wiping with a damp cloth does not remove the stain, spray a bit of white foaming shaving cream on the spot and let it set a few minutes. Rubbing alcohol also works. Rinse.

Leather/vinyl: Use a water-free dry-cleaning solvent according to the manufacturer's instructions. You may have to repeat application until the stain is gone. Finally, dry the spot with air from a fan.

Merthiolate

See the "Iodine and Metholide" section.

Milk

Carpet, fabric furniture, and mattresses: Apply an enzyme cleaner from the outside edges of the stain in, let it set for at least 15 minutes, and blot.

Alternatively, you can mix one part white vinegar to four parts water, and then saturate the carpet. Vinegar will remove the milk, but it's not as affective at removing the bacteria as an enzyme cleaner.

Laminated floors: Immediately blot, then clean with ¼ cup white vinegar per quart of water.

Wood floors: Wipe immediately. Use a terry towel and walk on it to help pull the moisture into the towel. Clean the floor with a small amount of an enzyme cleaner, then rinse and dry immediately. Pour cornstarch on the spot to absorb what moisture it can and remove the cornstarch. Set a fan on the floor and aim on the spot to help the liquid dry faster to prevent the boards from warping.

Wood furniture: Follow the directions for wood floors, only eliminate the fan. Allow the item to dry thoroughly and immediately apply a good wood cleaner and conditioner.

Leather/vinyl: Use a solution of 1 part bleach-free liquid enzyme laundry detergent to 30 parts water. Rinse by blotting with distilled water. Blot to remove excess water, and then dry with air from a fan.

Linoleum: Clean with ¼ cup white vinegar per quart of water.

Marble and granite: Clean with hot water and dry immediately.

Tile: Clean with an enzyme product, then again with plain hot water. Dry immediately.

Walls: Clean with an enzyme product to prevent any odor.

Mold/Mildew

Bathroom ceilings, tile, grout: Head to a medical supply store or beauty supply store for a bottle of 20 to 30 percent hydrogen peroxide. You may also need the activator if you purchase it at a beauty supply store. (Peroxide purchased in a drug or grocery store contains only 3 percent peroxide and isn't strong enough to kill mold.) Spray the peroxide on the mold. Wait 24 hours and repeat if necessary. Remember to remove towels before spraying. Peroxide is bleach and could discolor the towels or carpeting. Rinsing is not necessary.

Wood furniture: If possible, place the piece of furniture in the sun for several days, bringing the furniture inside at night. Again, peroxide is the safest product to use for killing mold on wood. Mix a 50/50 solution of 3 percent peroxide to water, wipe on, and rinse with a vinegar-and-water solution. Unfortunately, the peroxide will bleach the wood. Sanding and refinishing the wood is the best treatment for moldy wood.

Decks, siding, and roofs: The best method to remove mold on these surfaces is to rent a power washer. Spray the deck with a 50/50 solution of 20 percent hydrogen peroxide (medical supply stores and beauty supply stores carry it) and water to help prevent future mold buildup. For decks, rinse well to remove the peroxide. Otherwise the deck will need to be stained, which may be necessary anyway.

Carpet: Saturate the backing with 20 percent hydrogen peroxide, found at medical supply stores or beauty supply stores. (Be sure to ask whether their peroxide needs an activator.) Many janitorial supply stores also carry excellent mold-remediation products. Whatever product you use, open the windows and ventilate the room with a fan.

If you pull the carpet and padding and the flooring shows signs of mold, you must first kill the mold on the floor. After treating the mold, sand the floor and seal it before replacing the carpet. It may be wise to replace the carpet. Mold spores in carpet are difficult at best to completely kill. Many people have gone to hard surface flooring for this very reason.

Fabric furniture: First, remove loose mold from outer coverings of upholstered articles and mattresses. Do this outdoors, if possible, to prevent scattering mildew spores in the house. Wash the broom before reusing.

Run a vacuum cleaner attachment over the surface of the article to draw out more of the mold. If the vacuum has a disposable bag, remove and dispose of it immediately. If not, empty the bag carefully (preferably outdoors) to avoid scattering mold spores in the house.

If mildew remains, sponge lightly with the suds from a soap or detergent and wipe with a clean, damp cloth. Use as little water as possible so the filling does not get wet.

Another option is to wipe it with a cloth moistened with diluted alcohol (1 cup rubbing alcohol to 1 cup water). Dry the article thoroughly.

Mattresses: Spray the mattress with a solution of one part 20 percent hydrogen peroxide to three parts rubbing alcohol. Then let the mattress set in the sun all day, turning it once to expose both sides to the sunlight.

Laminated/wood floor: *For waxed finish:* The mold can usually be removed with a wood floor cleaning liquid and No. 1 steel wool.

For surface finishes: If mold is on the surface, wipe up with appropriate cleaner. If mold is under the finish, refinishing is necessary.

Linoleum: Gray splotchy areas in linoleum floors sometimes indicate mold growing up from the floorboards if there is a crack or leak in the plumbing or a mold problem underneath your home. Nothing will remove this mold from linoleum floors. You may need to replace the floorboards or sand and seal them before putting down new linoleum.

Leather/vinyl: Wipe with a cloth moistened with diluted alcohol (1 cup rubbing alcohol to 1 cup water). Dry in a current of air. If mildew remains, wash with thick suds made from a mild soap or detergent or a soap containing a germicide or fungicide. Then wipe with a damp cloth and dry in a current of air.

Unfinished Wood: Set the wood out in the sun all day to kill the mold. Wipe it with 3 percent peroxide, and rinse immediately. Then lightly sand the wood and treat it with a tung oil finish.

Mustard

See the "Coffee or Cola" section.

Nail Polish

Carpet, fabric furniture, and mattresses: Apply nail polish remover (acetone) and blot. Mix 1 teaspoon of a mild detergent containing no alkalis or bleaches with a cup of lukewarm water and blot. Rinse.

Laminated/wood floor: Rub gently with steel wool. After removing a stain, rinse the area thoroughly, dry completely, and, if floor finish has been removed in that area, recoat with appropriate finish or wax.

Leather/vinyl: First, dab a nonoily fingernail polish remover on an inconspicuous area of the item to test for colorfastness. If there's no damage, sponge the stained area with the polish remover until no more color is being removed. If nail polish remover damages the surface, use amyl acetate instead. If this doesn't work, sponge with alcohol (but test first). After it has dried, treat with a leather conditioner as the cleaners will dry the leather or vinyl, causing it to quickly crack if not properly conditioned.

Linoleum: Very carefully wipe with fingernail polish remover containing acetone (follow use instructions on label) on a clean white cloth.

Or rub with a cloth dampened in a concentrated detergent solution, or use scouring powder, water, and a plastic mesh pad.

If floor finish has been removed in that area, recoat with appropriate finish or wax.

Tile, marble, granite floors: Spray with Motsenbocker's Lift Off #3. Spray the stain thoroughly, wait at least 60 seconds, and then wipe with a clean towel. Repeat if necessary.

Walls: Spray with Motsenbocker's Lift Off #3. Spray the stain thoroughly, wait at least 60 seconds, and then wipe with a clean towel. Repeat if necessary.

Wood furniture: If the spilled polish is still wet, blot clean and wipe any remaining residue with mineral spirits. Avoid nail polish remover—it contains solvents that can dissolve the furniture finish. If the stain is dry, soak the stain for no longer than five minutes with boiled linseed oil, and then scrape off the residue with a nonstick spatula. Repeat the process as needed. Treat the wood after it dries with a wood conditioner to prevent drying and cracking of the wood.

Ointments

See the "Grease and Oil" section.

Paste Wax

On most surfaces, use a concentrated orange cleaner to dissolve the residue. Alternatively, hardware stores carry a product called DeSolvIt that works quite well on most surfaces.

Generously blot on the cleaner. Wait for an hour, and then blot (do not rub) to remove. Then apply liquid dishwashing soap to remove the cleaner and rinse with vinegar and water.

For wood furniture and wood flooring, contact a professional.

Paint: Latex, Water-Based Paints, and Art Paint

Carpet: Moisten the spot with hot water, and then squirt white foaming shaving cream onto the spot and let it set several hours. Remove what you can, blot, and then rinse. Or dab on denatured alcohol, wait an hour, and reapply. When the paint is softening, blot and reapply if needed. Rinse.

Fabric furniture and mattresses: Mix 1 teaspoon of a mild detergent containing no alkalis or bleaches with a cup of lukewarm water and blot it on the stain. Rinse. White foaming shaving cream will also work.

Laminated/wood floor: Scrub with a concentrated solution of detergent and water.

Leather/vinyl: Use denatured alcohol or white foaming shaving cream, following the instructions for carpet above.

Linoleum: Rub with a cloth or plastic mesh pad dipped in warm water and detergent.

Tile, marble, granite floors: Scrape off what you can with a plastic scraper, and then apply very hot water with a cloth, adding elbow grease. The StainEraser will remove paint from grout.

Pencil

Carpet, fabric furniture, and mattresses: First use a piece of boxing tape—not duct tape—doubled over to lift off as much of the pencil as possible. Then use a soft art eraser (the kind that can be molded, not a gum eraser). Rub it over the stain very gently and it should lift the pencil mark out. If any remains, clean with liquid dishwashing soap, blot, and rinse.

Tile, marble, granite floors: Rub gently with an art gum eraser.

Laminated/wood floor: Rub gently with an art gum eraser.

Leather/vinyl: Rub gently with an art gum eraser.

Linoleum: Rub gently with an art gum eraser.

Walls: Rub gently with an art gum eraser.

Wood furniture: Rub gently with an art gum eraser.

Wallpaper: Rub gently with an art gum eraser or commercial wallpaper cleaner. On washable paper, wipe with damp sponge, or sudsy sponge and then damp sponge if needed to remove the mark.

Petroleum Jelly

See the "Grease and Oil" section.

Popsicles and Punch

See the "Kool-Aid, Popsicles, Punch, and Grape Juice" section.

Rubber-Backed Throw Rugs

Unfortunately, the yellow stains left by these rugs on any floor surface are permanent. We recommend using only light-colored 100 percent cotton throw rugs with nonslip padding underneath them. If you do use these carpets, pick them up whenever any moisture lands on the carpet. Always pick them up after you shower and at night if they are in the kitchen. Watch closely for early signs of yellowing.

Rust

Carpet, fabric furniture, and mattresses: Squeeze enough juice from a fresh lemon to thoroughly saturate the spot. Generously sprinkle on some salt and let that set 24 hours, refreshing the lemon juice once or twice during that time. Rinse with cool water and repeat if needed.

Metal surfaces: Treat metal immediately. It's easier to treat a small spot than to sand and repaint. Naval jelly dissolves small rust spots. WD-40 and DeSolvIt work quite well. There are also several excellent rust removers available at hardware stores. After the rust has been removed, rinse with sudsy water, dry thoroughly, and paint with a rust preventive paint.

Porcelain and fiberglass: Rub the stain with a cut lemon, or apply lemon juice. If the fixture is badly stained, use a 5 percent solution of oxalic acid or a 10 percent solution of hydrochloric acid. Apply the acid solution with a cloth and leave it on only a second or two, and then rinse it off thoroughly. (Be sure to protect your skin and eyes by wearing rubber or plastic gloves and protective goggles! Ventilate the room well by opening windows and turning on the fan.)

Laminated/wood floor and linoleum: Use a commercial rust remover made for your type of floor. If steel wool is suggested, use 000 grade.

Leather/vinyl: See the "Carpet Stain-Removal Guidelines" section.

Tile, marble, granite floors: Use a commercial rust remover. Follow directions exactly and do not leave on surface very long, because acid in many rust removers can etch the surface.

Walls: Use either naval jelly or CLR, found at most hardware stores. Prime and repaint if needed.

Wood furniture: Try applying the juice from a fresh lemon as you would for carpet. Do not allow it to set for long or it will warp the wood. Blot. If that begins to dissolve the rust, wait 24 to 48 hours for the wood to dry and repeat. If the rust is stubborn, boil linseed oil (open the windows and turn on a fan), lightly apply to the wood, wait 5 to 10 minutes, and blot. The wood may need to be sanded with a 0000 steel-wool pad. Then apply a wood conditioner or refinish if needed.

Salad Dressing

See the "Grease and Oil" section.

Sap

Automobile: Using a petroleum distillate on a car will remove the sealant. Apply baby oil or vegetable oil and give it an hour to loosen the sap. Repeat if needed. If this does not remove the sap, use mineral oil. Rinse immediately using a damp, soft cotton cloth and a squirt of liquid dishwashing soap. Then rinse with a vinegar-and-water solution followed by plain water.

Clothing, furniture, and decks: Often the oil from peanut butter will remove tree sap. Dab on a good bit of it, giving it an hour to loosen the sap. Repeat if needed. If that doesn't work, try DeSolvIt, which is found at various department stores.

Hair or hands: Gently rub baby oil or vegetable oil on the sap. Give the oil 5 to 10 minutes to loosen the sap and wash with warm sudsy water. Repeat if needed. A nonabrasive hand cleaner called Go Jo (available at automotive stores) also does a good job on tree sap as well as oil and grease. Rub in and give it 15 to 30 minutes to work, and then thoroughly rinse with vinegar and water.

Scorch Marks

Scorch marks made by irons, cigarette burns, or other forms of heat are not removable. They are burned into the fabric or surface.

If the mark is in wood and is very light, try buffing with a good wax and plenty of elbow grease. Work in the direction of the grain.

Shoe Polish

Carpet: Sponge with a small amount of dry-cleaning solvent, and then blot. Mix 1 teaspoon of a mild detergent containing no alkalis or bleaches with 1 cup of lukewarm water. Blot it on, and then rinse.

Laminated/wood floors and wood furniture: The polish works into the grain of the wood and will be impossible to completely remove. First try blotting the polish with rubbing alcohol. Wait 15 minutes and blot to remove. Alcohol removes some shoe polishes but not all of them.

If that does not bring the desired results, apply a bit of turpentine. If the polish remains, it has soaked into the grain and the wood must be sanded and refinished.

Fabric furniture and mattresses: Try blotting with rubbing alcohol, and then use DeSolvIt, which is found at hardware stores. Apply, wait 30 minutes, rinse with sudsy water, and then rinse with vinegar and water.

Leather/vinyl: Contact the manufacturer for instructions.

Soot

Fireplace fronts: First wash the bricks with a strong detergent like Non TSP (found at most paint stores) and a good stiff-bristle brush. After cleaning (be sure to put down plastic to protect all surfaces), spray the bricks thoroughly with a can of foaming bath cleaner. Saturate the bricks thoroughly and wait 30 minutes, and then wash again with the Non TSP. Bricks are very porous, and most cleaners saturate through the bricks. A foaming bath cleaner adheres to the surface of the bricks, giving the cleaner time to dissolve the soot.

Walls: A chemically treated dry sponge quickly removes soot from walls without leaving a residue. The sponge is used dry and wiped across the wall. This is the same way professional cleaners wipe down walls after a house fire.

Fabric furniture: First wipe the furniture with a chemically treated dry sponge. Use the sponge dry and keep moving it so as not to spread the soot to other parts of the item. Then clean the item with a foaming furniture cleaner, testing an inconspicuous spot first.

Stickers

Cars: Grab your hair dryer and heat the sticker until the adhesive softens and the sticker can be removed with a cloth dampened in sudsy water.

Plastic: Apply dry-cleaning fluid. Allow the fluid to remain on the label only long enough to allow the label to be rubbed off. Wipe away excess fluid immediately, and wash article in sudsy water and dry.

> **Dishing the Dirt**
>
> Never use ammonia on plastic or aluminum. Ammonia will interact chemically with either material, and can "burn" the aluminum or plastic.

Glass, mirrors, and metals other than aluminum: Fold a paper towel or cloth to make a thick pad as large as the label. Dampen the pad with household ammonia and lay it over the label. (Use masking tape to hold pad onto a vertical surface.) Wait a half hour to two hours, redampening the pad if it dries out. The label will slide off.

Aluminum: Heat with a hair dryer and wipe off. If any residue remains, use a metal polish such as Met-All or Flitz to remove the rest.

Suntan Lotion

See the "Grease and Oil" section.

Tar

See the "Glue and Adhesive" section.

Urine

Carpet and Mattresses: When urine hits the padding in carpet, it spreads. What looks like a small stain on the surface is twice that large on the padding. Always treat an area two to three times as large as the surface stain, otherwise the odor remains and the pet continues to return to the same spot. Pour on plenty of an enzyme cleaner such as Bac-Out, which is an enzyme product that not only gets rid of the stain but banishes the odor as well. The enzymes "eat" the odor-causing bacteria.

Fabric furniture: Remove as much of the urine from the couch as you can with a wet or dry vac. Then soak the seat cushion with Bac-Out. If that doesn't work, you may need to replace the padding in your fabric furniture.

Laminated/wood floor: Rub with a hot, damp cloth and scouring powder. For old, stubborn stains, use a 10-to-1 solution of water and liquid bleach. Rinse well with clean water.

Leather/vinyl: Use a solution of 1 part bleach-free liquid enzyme laundry detergent to 30 parts water. Rinse by blotting with distilled water. Blot to remove excess water, and then dry with air from a fan.

Vomit

See the "Urine" section.

Water Spots

Carpet: Mix a thin paste of baking soda and 3 percent hydrogen peroxide. Gently blot on the spot. Wait 30 minutes and spray with straight peroxide. Allow to dry, brush off what you can, and vacuum to remove the rest. Repeat if needed. Rinse with the vinegar-and-water solution.

Fabric furniture and mattresses: Pour a bit of baking soda on the spot, and then spray with 3 percent hydrogen peroxide. Wait 30 minutes and spray again with peroxide. Wait until the baking soda has dried, and then rinse. Repeat if needed. Sometimes water stains on fabric furniture can be removed with straight 3 percent hydrogen peroxide.

Glass shower doors: Open the window, turn on a fan, and ventilate the room. Bring some white vinegar to a boil. Put on a pair of rubber gloves and, with a clean sponge, thoroughly saturate the glass door with the vinegar. Keep repeating this every 15 minutes for an hour. Dampen a white scrub pad (do not use any other color pad as they are more aggressive and will scratch the glass) with the vinegar and add some baking soda to the pad. Scrub the door.

This should remove the whitish look of the water spots. It may need to be repeated depending on the severity of the spots. Remember when water is allowed to stand on a surface, the alkali etches into the surface. The etching is permanent and cannot be removed. A bar of kaolin clay, which is used for removing impurities from cars, might also help to remove the water spots.

Laminated/wood floors: Water damage on hardwood floors generally happens because a pet urinates on the floor or the water has run over after watering a plant. Laminated floors do not stain as easily as wood floors. Absorb as much moisture as possible with a terry towel. Then pour cornstarch on the spot to absorb even more. Press the cornstarch into the floor and replace it with fresh cornstarch as it becomes moistened.

Linoleum: Water damage will look gray or nearly black as it does in wood floors. It cannot be removed from linoleum floors.

Marble and granite: Unless marble and granite are dried immediately after spilling liquid on the floor or damp mopping, water spots will form on the surface. They will look just like water spots on windows and glass shower doors. Try gently buffing the floor with kaolin clay. Make certain the clay you purchase is 100 percent kaolin clay and does not contain any other chemicals. Kaolin clay is solid. If the clay you find is in liquid form, it contains other chemicals that will damage the floor.

Should the water spots refuse to budge, contact Fred Hueston at www.ntc-stone.com. Fred is a leading expert in stone floor care and will have a product that safely removes water spots from marble or granite.

Windows: See the advice for glass shower doors in this section.

Wax

Always place a candle on a candleholder. Candles sweat and leave stains on any hard surface. Never move a burning candle; wait until the wax has solidified. Burn smokeless candles only.

Candlesticks: Place in the freezer for one to two hours. The wax chips right off.

Clothing: Freeze the wax with ice in a zip-lock bag. Chip off as much wax as possible with a plastic scraper. Place the clothing on top of a paper bag with no printing, and then put an all-white paper towel on top of the wax. Set the iron to medium and iron over the wax. The iron melts the wax into the paper bag. (If you use a paper towel or bag with printing, the heat from the iron sets the ink into the fabric.) To remove the color from colored wax, try soaking the garment in straight 3 percent hydrogen peroxide overnight.

Carpet, mattresses, and fabric furniture: Freeze the wax first with an ice cube placed in a zip-lock bag and scrape off what you can with a plastic scraper. Grab an all-white paper towel. Set your hair dryer to the hottest setting and heat the wax, wiping it up with the paper towel as it melts. Do not use an iron on carpet. Many carpets are made from Olefin, which is polyester or plastic. It does not take long for the heat from an iron to leave ugly scorch marks in the carpet. A hair dryer may take a bit longer, but it works and is quite safe to use.

Laminated/wood floor and wood furniture: Place a piece of waxed paper over the wax and set your iron to medium hot. Iron the wax for a few seconds. The wax from the waxed paper melts the wax and lifts it from the surface. If a strain remains, you may be able to remove it with hydrogen peroxide or a remover found at candle shops.

Leather/vinyl: Freezing leather and vinyl is the only safe way to remove wax from these surfaces. Any solvents used on either surface will discolor and damage the fabric. If there is a dye stain left after the wax is removed, pour a bit of baking soda on the spot, and then spray with hydrogen peroxide. The mixture will bubble and fizzle, and sometimes you get lucky and the stain will come out. Let the mixture set on the dye for 15 minutes and rinse. If it doesn't come out, leave the stain alone. Any solvent, soap, or detergent will further damage the leather or vinyl.

Linoleum: Freeze with an ice cube in a zip-lock bag and scrape off the hardened wax with a plastic scraper. Use a hair dryer set to medium heat to remove any wax that worked down into those little divots. Beware! Any dye left in the floor is permanent. It has seeped into the inner layers and will not come out.

Tile, marble, granite floors: For granite and marble floors, follow the instructions for linoleum floors. For tile floors, freeze as you would for linoleum floors. Melted wax will penetrate into the open "spores" of the tile. Heating the wax will only drive it deeper into the tile. Instead, boil some water and then place the pan next to you on a hot pad on the floor. Wearing a pair of rubber gloves, dip a clean, soft cloth in the boiling water and immediately apply to the wax. Sometimes the wax will melt into the cloth. Keep a dry cloth handy for fast blotting.

Walls: You can't remove wax from a wall without damaging the wallboard. The safest method is to beg a friend for assistance. Drape a clean cloth over a dust pan and place that immediately under the wax with no wall space between the pad and the wax. This will catch the wax as it drips. Hold a second cloth in your other hand to blot the wax as it melts. Begin heating the wax gently on the low setting of a hair dryer. As the wax melts, catch what you can with the towel you are holding. The dust pan and cloth will scoop up the rest. If a dye stain remains (and it will), seal the wall with a primer and repaint.

Wine

Carpet: For spills that are noticed immediately, blot quickly, and then pour a bit of white wine or seltzer water on the spot.

Blot 3 percent hydrogen peroxide on the spot, and then wait five minutes. Blot on more peroxide if needed, and then rinse.

Missed the stain? Mix a 50/50 solution of hydrogen peroxide to water. Spray it on the spot and let it set 15 minutes. Rinse. Repeat if needed. Wine stains that have gone untreated on the carpet may take several treatments to remove.

Fabric furniture: Dampen a clean, white cloth with hydrogen peroxide. Begin at the outer edge of the stain and blot working toward the center of the stain. This will help prevent the stain from spreading. Wait 10 minutes, and then rinse. Repeat if needed.

Laminated/wood floor: Wipe immediately to prevent the wine from seeping deep into the wood. After wiping, pour some cornstarch onto the stain and press it into the wood. Sweep up and keep applying the cornstarch until the moisture is gone. It's best to leave any stain alone.

Adding more moisture at this point may result not only in dark stain, but it may warp the wood as well. Call in a professional.

Leather/vinyl: Dampen a white paper towel with hydrogen peroxide and lay it on the spot, weighing it down with something heavy such as a pan for 30 minutes. If the stain has improved but still remains, repeat. Mix a paste of baking soda and hydrogen peroxide and gently rub to remove any stain left in the crevices. White foaming shaving cream may also help to remove the remaining stain. Finally, treat the leather with a good conditioner.

Linoleum: Wipe immediately. If the wine seeps into the linoleum, the stain is permanent. Sometimes an oven cleaner will remove deep stains in linoleum. Just be aware that it will remove the wax from the floor. You can strip and rewax the floor if needed.

Mattresses: Mix a paste of baking soda and hydrogen peroxide and plaster it on the spot. Wait 30 minutes and spray with straight peroxide. Let it dry and wipe off the baking soda. Repeat if needed.

Marble and granite: Wipe off with warm water and dry immediately. Granite and marble generally don't stain.

Tile: Apply hydrogen peroxide to the stain and rinse with a towel saturated with hot water, and then dry immediately. After the red wine has seeped into the tile, there's little you can do to remove the stain. You can remove red wine stains in grout with The StainEraser.

Walls: Dab on a bit of hydrogen peroxide. If the stain remains, you need to apply a primer and repaint the wall.

Wood furniture: Blot immediately until no more moisture has soaked into the towel. Press cornstarch on the stain to absorb as much wine as possible. Remove and repeat until the moisture is gone. Wait until the wood has dried, and then apply peroxide. It may be possible to apply a wood stain or use the meat of a walnut or pecan to restore the color. Sanding and refinishing the surface may be necessary.

Appendix B

Resources

Not sure where to get kaolin clay? Or carnauba wax? Check out these resources for finding the products we mention in this book.

AURO All Purpose Cleaner: www.sinanco.com

Bac Out: Health food stores or www.goclean.com/bac-out.htm.

Bi-O-Kleen: Health food stores and www.goclean.com/bio-kleen.htm.

Bio Ox: Contact the manufacturer for an outlet near you at www.Bio-Ox.com or 1-866-246-6943.

Bon Ami Cleaning Powder: Any supermarket.

Carnauba wax: Automotive supply stores or www.autogeek.net.

Denatured alcohol: Ask a pharmacist.

DeSolvIt: Wal-Mart, Kmart, department stores, or www.dtep.com/buy-de-solv-it.htm.

Dry sponge: Kitchen and bath stores or www.goclean.com/dry-sponge.htm.

Ecover products: To find a distributor near you, go to www.ecover.com.

Enzyme products: See Nature's Miracle or Bac Out.

Erase It for Bathrooms: www.goclean.com/erase-it.htm.

Flitz: Automotive supply stores, 1-800-333-9325, or www.flitz-polish.com.

Guardsman Furniture Polish: Fine furniture stores.

Horsehair brush: Restaurant supply stores or fine clothing stores.

Hydrogen peroxide, 3 percent: Grocery stores and drug stores.

Hydrogen peroxide, 20 percent: Medical supply stores.

Ion-A-Clean: www.goclean.com/ion-clean.htm.

Kaolin clay: Automotive supply stores.

Lambswool duster: Kitchen and bath supply stores and department stores, or www.drugstore.com.

Leather cleaner and conditioner: Western supply stores or www. leathermagic.com.

Life Tree Automatic Dishwashing Liquid: Natural food stores or 1-800.824.6396.

Met All: Automotive supply stores; or, to find a dealer near you, call 1-800-835-5578 or visit www.met-all.com.

Motsenbocker's Lift Off #3: Home centers. Or, to order through DutchGuard.com, call 1-800-821-5157 or visit www.dutchguard.com/ p-LIFTOFF3.html.

Naturally Yours All Purpose Cleaner: www.naturallyyoursstore.com/ id2.html

Nature's Miracle: Pet stores or www.PETsMART.com.

Naval jelly: Hardware stores or home centers.

Non TSP: Paint stores.

Plastic scraper: Kitchen supply stores or www.goclean.com/accessories. htm#scrape.

Restorz-It: www.restorz-it.com or 1-800-759-4345.

Squeegee: Hardware stores or www.goclean.com/accessories.htm#ws.

The StainEraser: To find a dealer near you, visit www.thestaineraser.com or call 1-888-387-6111.

Zep: Home centers.

Index

D

MARY MOPPINS

CLEANING SYSTEM

"It's not clean until it's Mary Moppins clean!"